How to Wholesale Real Estate

How to
Wholesale Real Estate

The No-Cash Strategy to Build a Scalable Business

Jamil Damji

BiggerPockets®
PUBLISHING
Denver, Colorado

Praise for
How to
Wholesale Real Estate

"When I first started, Jamil was one of the most instrumental people in my real estate career. To this day, I still rely on him. This book will change your life…just as Jamil has changed my and my family's lives. No one knows wholesaling better than Jamil Damji!"

—PACE MORBY, *Wall Street Journal* best-selling author of *Wealth without Cash*

"Jamil masterfully breaks down the concepts of ethical wholesaling and scaling a sustainable real estate business in what I now consider to be the Unofficial Wholesaling Bible."

—ROB ABASOLO, host of the *BiggerPockets Real Estate Podcast*

"If you want to learn to wholesale real estate, you need to read this book. Jamil is the best in the business and an amazing teacher."

—DAVE MEYER, best-selling author of *Real Estate by the Numbers* and host of the *On the Market* podcast

"No one in this industry knows wholesale real estate better than Jamil. If you're looking to go from your first deal to a thriving six- or seven-figure business, this book is the blueprint to get you there!"

—JERRY NORTON, flipping genius and CEO of Flipping Mastery

"Jamil Damji is the best wholesaler I have ever seen, but what sets Jamil apart is his genuine desire to help others succeed. This book is a testament to his commitment to sharing his knowledge and experience. If you are looking to generate life-changing income through wholesaling, then you have come to the right place!"

—HENRY WASHINGTON, cohost of
the *On the Market* podcast

"I've witnessed Jamil's real estate prowess firsthand, and he's a powerhouse. He's more energetic than a toddler on a sugar rush, his passion for real estate is infectious, and he loves his community more than the tastiest chicken wings. When he told me he was writing a book about wholesaling, I knew it would be a winner. And boy, did he deliver! This book is loaded with secrets, tips, and tricks that even the most experienced wholesalers will find valuable. It's like having a secret weapon at your disposal."

—BRAD HOLCMAN, Senior Director, A&E Unscripted
and Alternative Programming

How to Wholesale Real Estate: The No-Cash Strategy to Build a Scalable Business
Jamil Damji

Published by BiggerPockets Publishing LLC, Denver, CO
Copyright © 2023 by Jamil Damji
All rights reserved.

Publisher's Cataloging-in-Publication Data
Names: Damji, Jamil, author.
Title: How to wholesale real estate : the no cash strategy to build a scalable business / Jamil Damji
Description: Denver, CO: BiggerPockets Publishing, LLC, 2023.
Identifiers: ISBN: 9781947200920 (paperback) | 9781947200937 (ebook)
Subjects: LCSH Real estate investment--United States. | Personal finance. | Investments. | BISAC BUSINESS & ECONOMICS / Real Estate / Buying & Selling Homes | BUSINESS & ECONOMICS / Real Estate / General | BUSINESS & ECONOMICS / Investments & Securities / Real Estate | BUSINESS & ECONOMICS / Personal Finance / Investing
Classification: LCC HD1382.5 .D36 2023 | DDC 332.63/24--dc23

Printed in Canada on recycled paper
MBP 10 9 8 7 6 5 4 3 2 1

Dedication

I dedicate this book to the most meaningful people in my life. The ones who have sacrificed everything to help get me to this position in life. Without you, none of this would be possible.

To my mom and dad, Nurjehan and Anil Damji. Your love and sacrifice are the reasons your children flourished. We love you so much. Thank you for showing us how to live with love and God as our guide.

To my wife, Natalie Gallant, and my girls Karisma and Tayla. Thank you for being the foundation of my life. I'm always trying to make you proud of me. I know I'm corny sometimes, but it's pretty cool that your husband and dad is a published author!

To my sister, Rahima Blaza. Thank you so much for being the greatest friend, protector, partner, and champion in my life. Even when I messed it all up at times, you picked me up and we carried forward.

To my incredible business partners Josiah Grimes, Hunter Runyon, Rahima Blaza, and Nick Fisher. Wow!! Look what we did. We took a broken industry and put the heart back in it. I'm forever grateful for you all.

To my best friend Pace Morby. Thank you for teaching me what it really means to give. Your heart is bigger than the earth!

Lastly, to our Creator. You took a little kid with a dream in his heart and led him to the greatest life ever. I'm humbled. God is Great.

Table of Contents

SECTION I
Understanding the Basics of Wholesaling

SECTION II
Building Up Your Wholesale Business

SECTION III
Scaling a Wholesaling Empire

Preface

You may be wondering why I have the authority to write this book and what you can learn from it.

I've been revolutionizing the world of real estate for over twenty years. I cofounded KeyGlee, one of the fastest growing real estate franchise businesses in the United States, which is heavily involved in the world of wholesaling. With hundreds of franchises across the United States, our gross revenue in 2022 was $38 million, with a gross profit of $18.4 million. I've completed over five thousand transactions and am involved with sixty to eighty transactions monthly, not including franchises.

Along with my deep success in wholesaling, I am the main host on the A&E show *Triple Digit Flip*. I teach new and seasoned real estate investors how to wholesale in AstroFlipping, my real estate education course. BiggerPockets recently named me as the subject matter expert for wholesaling, and I'm a panelist on the Bigger-Pockets *On the Market* podcast. I'm the host of *Wholesale Hotline*, a real estate podcast that teaches new investors how to get their first wholesaling deal. I was featured in *Forbes* and actively contribute to Forbes Council posts.

Wholesale real estate investing has been my No. 1 strategy to grow two thriving seven-figure businesses and generate millions of dollars in wealth. Now, with this book, I want to teach you how to do the same.

What is wholesale real estate? Simply, wholesale is a form of real estate investing in which you act as a *principal* in a transaction. In real estate, a principal is the contractual party in a transaction, either as the buyer or the seller. *A principal is not a representative for anyone else but acts solely as the buyer or the seller in the contract.* In traditional real estate, a wholesaler is not a principal because that person represents the principal, whether that's the buyer or the seller. For wholesalers, the aim is to find properties and opportunities where there's a potential for forced appreciation, which you sell directly to another principal (buyer) who proactively increases the value of a property. Examples of forced appreciation include:

- Adding carpeting to floors.
- Renovating kitchens with new fixtures and upgraded materials.
- Adding pools in backyards.
- Changing the zoning of property, such as splitting lots, combining lots, etc.

You sell your rights or equitable interest in that contract to a buyer who will realize the future potential of the property. Wholesalers are paid through the fees we collect for finding the properties. Examples of principals who buy wholesale property include:

- Developers.
- Buy-and-hold investors.
- Fix-and-flippers.
- Institutional buyers.
- Tax strategists.

The key to being a successful wholesaler is learning to locate opportunities and sell that potential to another principal. What you seek is value. If you can spot and create value, you have the potential to make a tremendous amount of money. There will always be opportunities for wholesaling no matter the economic conditions or the state of the real estate market.

For example, as of the writing of this book, the real estate market has fundamentally changed; some say for the worse. Seasoned real estate investors, however, know that downturns in the market are incredible opportunities to buy properties at a substantial discount. Compared to when the market is highly competitive, downturns are the perfect time to buy. The key to success, even in a downturn market, is to know the right strategies and how to identify potentially valuable opportunities.

You may be asking yourself, "Why now, Jamil? Why is now the time to get started with real estate investing?"

Simply, the market has shifted significantly. Interest rates have spiked while affordability for purchasing a home is at an all-time low. As a result, there has been a significant decrease in prospects from the buying pool. This in turn has created more downward pressure on pricing, so truly motivated sellers are willing to sell at a discount. This has transitioned us from a longtime seller's market to a buyer's market.

This gives wholesalers a unique opportunity right now. Previously, wholesalers had a hard time convincing homeowners to sell at realistic prices for homes in distressed conditions, often facing unrealistic discussions about the value. This left wholesalers either priced out of opportunities or facing months of difficult negotiations.

However, this market shift also means there are fewer motivated buyers, which gives a potential buyer more leverage in making deals. Working with a wholesaler might even be the best option for this type of homeowner, particularly those looking to sell on an expedited timeline because of a life situation such as relocation for work, a medical event, or a divorce.

Here's an example of a situation I encountered in 2018. A real estate agent approached me with a listing that she was having a hard time selling. This listing was a custom mansion in the Arcadia neighborhood of Phoenix, Arizona. This home had been sitting on the Multiple Listing Service (MLS) for nine months at $900,000. It had started at $1 million but the agent steadily dropped the price over that time.

The agent didn't have a solution for the homeowner, who was under tremendous financial pressure to sell the home in addition to grieving the passing of his wife. All he wanted was the money from the sale of the property so he could go live near his kids and start a new chapter in his life. It didn't look to me like this property could be sold for $900,000 either.

However, I realized that this mansion sat on a one-acre plot of land in a highly sought-after development and it had perfect zoning options. I saw the potential of the property. It was not the custom mansion, but the land itself. Nobody else thought to demolish the mansion, so I presented the property to a developer who wanted to subdivide the acre to build five new homes on it.

The parties locked up the deal at $900,000 after all; the land (and the mansion) were sold to the developer, and I made a $100,000 assignment fee. More importantly, the seller could finally move on with his life after nine months of no sales. Plus, the real estate agent made a handsome commission. All of this happened because I looked at the situation from a different perspective, saw the potential, and sold that potential to a developer.

Your job as a successful wholesaler is to hunt for this kind of potential and understand all of the use cases for real estate, just as I did in 2018. That's the reason I wrote this book. I want to dispel the stigma many wholesalers face, to explain where a wholesaler's profit comes from, and to provide an ethical framework on how wholesale operations can be profitable and add value to the lives and businesses of the people we work with.

To be honest, I got into wholesaling by accident, and believe me that I've made my share of mistakes. The secret was to turn all of my mistakes into learning opportunities, which led me to become one of the best wholesalers in the industry. The foundation of wholesaling is understanding value and how to spot it. Using wholesale as your primary strategy, you can generate cash that can then be used for more real estate investing.

In this book, I will teach you the basics of wholesale, its legalities and ethics, how to build a business, how to generate leads and sales without betting the bank, and finally how to scale your business into a multimillion-dollar empire.

Are you ready?

Let's go!

SECTION I
Understanding the Basics of Wholesaling

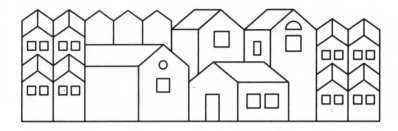

CHAPTER 1
Why Wholesale?

In 2008, the housing market was in a free fall; when it crashed, it unearthed the many inefficiencies, predatory practices, and opportunities for regulation. This ultimately made the housing market substantially safer than it had been. Leading up to the crash, I had been primarily wholesaling. I began my career by wholesaling single-family properties and graduated into apartment complexes. It wasn't until I pivoted again into multifamily development that I exposed myself to risks that not only financially ruined me but also family members who believed in me so much that they blindly and personally guaranteed millions of dollars in leverage.

Everything got foreclosed, including my and my family members' homes. We lost the house I grew up in and all our vehicles; our bank accounts were frozen to protect creditors; and I personally lost $12 million in a matter of months. I tell this story because there is a lot of pain in the real estate market. Some economists and news outlets have made parallels between what we're seeing in the current market and what happened in 2008.

Understanding the Changing Wholesale Landscape

The real estate market right now is a new frontier. Changes in monetary policy and rising interest rates have engineered a market shift by reducing buyer demand in one of the most unaffordable markets in the history of U.S. housing. The Fed made a steep interest rate change in summer 2022, going up 55 basis points, which was the biggest change week over week since 1987. It then increased the rate again by 75 basis points in the same time period. The speed of the rate hikes was an emergency response to unfettered inflation, some of which was related to housing, such as material costs of goods, maintenance, and supply chain challenges caused by the COVID-19 pandemic. The average American household experienced dramatically decreased purchasing power in a matter of months. In layman's terms in real estate, you either can afford less house or pay more for the same house than when it hit the market.

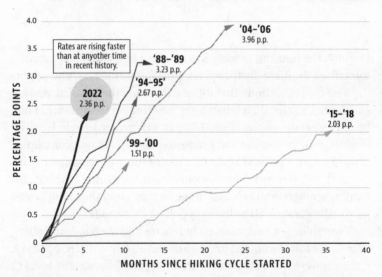

COMPARING THE SPEED OF U.S. INTEREST RATE HIKES

Rates are rising faster than at anyother time in recent history.

2022
2.36 p.p.

'88-'89
3.23 p.p.

'94-'95'
2.67 p.p.

'04-'06
3.96 p.p.

'15-'18
2.03 p.p.

'99-'00
1.51 p.p.

PERCENTAGE POINTS

MONTHS SINCE HIKING CYCLE STARTED

Source: visualcapitalist.com

When comparing the housing market now to what happened in 2008, what we're seeing is a correction, and not another housing crash. A correction means home prices drop slightly, usually 10 percent or less; what is happening as of early 2023, during the writing of this book, is a national average drop of around 5 to 7 percent. In 2008 there was a staggering drop of more than 30 percent, which is evidence of a housing crash. A correction can last from six months to over a year; the housing market experienced a similar correction at the end of 2018 and start of 2019.

It's important to note that the United States doesn't have one single housing market. Different regions are affected locally, so it's important to study data specific to whatever market you want to invest in. Market fluctuations don't necessarily mean investors should be worried or hold onto their dollars until the storm passes. It does mean that investors must rely on the fundamentals of real estate investing to take advantage of unique times with extraordinary potential.

I reentered the real estate game after I lost that $12 million in 2008. The difference in 2010 was that the housing market had hit rock bottom and had only one way to go: up. Few people were buying real estate because the average person was staying away from "toxic" asset classes. I could buy properties at a fraction of their peak value. Between 2010 and 2012, I purchased $800,000 worth of property in Phoenix, Arizona (my specialty area). In 2019, I exited those same properties for $8 million. That was a 10x return on investment by taking advantage of a market shift and getting back to the fundamentals of real estate.

I cherry-picked properties, this time looking for the best buy-and-hold opportunities. I looked to generate the cash required to fund these types of opportunities. That's the power of wholesale in shifting markets: You have the advantage of generating cash, spotting opportunities, and executing when those deals present themselves. My good friend and real estate aficionado Dolf de Roos says in his book *Real Estate Riches* that "the deal of a decade comes around once a week." A good wholesaler first has the cash on hand to take advantage of these opportunities.

Why Wholesale Is Perfect for New Investors

To recap, wholesale real estate investing is a strategy in which you secure the contractual rights to purchase a property with the potential for forced appreciation. You then sell those contractual rights to someone who will realize that potential. The best thing about wholesaling is you never buy the property. (Which means even with limited funds, you could do this.)

Wholesaling is a viable strategy in any market condition. In a bear market, everyone wants to buy real estate at the low point, so wholesalers are key for other buyers because of our ability to find real estate. Wholesalers add value to the economy in a bear market by contributing volume in the marketplace, especially when retail buyers have stepped out of the picture. In so-called flat markets, wholesalers can find golden opportunities because there's a plethora of real estate deals. Wholesalers are the experts who find the hidden pearls. Meanwhile, in a bull market, we're the ones who can negotiate deep discounts. As prices go sky-high in bull markets, we bring in opportunities for others.

Wholesaling is lucrative because it allows you to sell an opportunity without investing large amounts of time or money into the renovation or sale of the home. Many beginner real estate investors use this strategy to generate cash to fund future real estate investment goals. There are four reasons why wholesale is such an attractive strategy for new investors:

1. You can start wholesaling today in most states, even without a real estate license (in some states, you do need a license).
2. You don't need much money or credit to get started.
3. You don't need previous real estate experience.
4. You encounter significantly less risk than with other real estate strategies.

I next go into each of these four points in more detail.

1. YOU CAN START WHOLESALING TODAY

Starting off as a wholesaler is a perfect way to build a foundation in the fundamentals of real estate. From here, you can, for example, branch out as a fix-and-flip real estate agent or go into buy-and-hold properties. The best part? In most states, you don't need a real estate license to get started. (More on this in Chapter 3.) For example, I do not have a real estate license yet have successfully closed thousands of deals. However, I require everybody else at my company to be licensed because I prefer to be safe than sorry.

Whether you're licensed or not, a crucial piece to getting started is understanding the value of a property. In the industry, this is done through underwriting, which is commonly known as comping (discussed in Chapter 6). Underwriting is doing the necessary research on the value of a property. Understanding the value of a property uses appraisal rules.

The appraisal rules are simply the rules that all appraisers follow when evaluating properties. To understand how appraisers determine value, I informally interviewed hundreds of appraisers. I can't stress enough how important it is to learn and follow these rules.

Knowing how to value and compare properties separates the good wholesalers from the best wholesalers. Accurately evaluating a property and doing it well makes you indispensable to investors, other wholesalers, fix-and-flippers, and real estate agents in your area. I feel so strongly about the importance of comping that I freely share the list of appraisal rules. I post them on my Instagram account and I host a weekly show about them. These rules are crucial to understanding the ins and outs of all real estate business.

2. YOU DON'T NEED MUCH MONEY OR CREDIT

A common misconception about real estate investing is that you need a lot of money to get started. (In the more traditional ways that investors find leads and new deals, that belief isn't entirely unfounded.) My first wholesaling deal that I was responsible for managing netted me $50,000. It was because I lived around the area that property developers were interested in, not because I spent thousands of dollars on marketing to bring potential deals to my doorstep. That $50,000 sale turned into a $47,0000 payday, with the remaining amount paying for various fees.

Now, you might be thinking that purchasing a home and an

investment property are different, and you'd be correct. But even if you don't have the tens of thousands of dollars to purchase a property, you can still get started in real estate investing without using your personal savings or credit. Because of the quick turnaround time for wholesale deals to generate cash flow, this is a system that doesn't require your money to be put down. In this landscape, this method has a low level of financial risk while potentially offering a high financial reward.

3. YOU DON'T NEED PREVIOUS REAL ESTATE EXPERIENCE

You don't need previous experience either as a real estate investor or in running a real estate business. Don't get me wrong. These types of experience help, but you don't need them to flourish as a wholesaler. As noted earlier, being a wholesaler may not require you to have a real estate license or any type of official certification. Rather than spending weeks or months of intensive study to start doing deals, in many states you could start quickly through wholesaling.

Also as noted earlier, I am a big proponent of having a license, even though I don't have one. The benefit of having a license is discussed in Chapter 3. You might even decide to get one after you start wholesale investing. I do see the many benefits that are afforded to those with a license, which is why I require new hires at KeyGlee to already have their licenses.

It's important to keep in mind that some states require licenses for wholesale activity. I point out here that the lack of a license requirement makes wholesale attractive to new investors entering the market because of the flexibility and speed with which they can start and close deals.

4. YOU ENCOUNTER SIGNIFICANTLY LESS RISK

So, I bet you're wondering, "Jamil, now I know the benefits of wholesaling, but what kind of returns can I expect when I start closing deals?"

Despite the recent disruptions in the housing market, my business has flourished, as I discussed earlier. The catch is that there is potential *if* you know the kinds of proven strategies that generate those kinds of profits. I'll outline those strategies in the following chapters, but my experience shows that wholesalers can mitigate risk, regardless of the housing climate. If you're just starting out in real estate investing, the returns from wholesale strategies are ideal to help you get established in real estate and to build relationships.

This also lets you open the door for future experimentation within real estate, especially with your newly honed skills of identifying a property's potential and learning how to find deals without the burden of expensive marketing costs. Wholesale is truly a powerful strategy, but for too long it's had a bad reputation and years of misconceptions, leading curious investors to avoid the strategy altogether. Don't worry: In the next chapter we'll look at some of the misconceptions and how to dispel them.

A QUICK RECAP

- Wholesale real estate investing is a strategy in which you secure rights to a property that has the opportunity to force appreciation because of its potential and you sell that potential to a buyer for a profit.
- Current market influences are related to the aftermath of the pandemic, to ongoing supply chain challenges, and to constant federal interest rate hikes in 2023.
- The current market presents an incredible opportunity for new investors to enter wholesale real estate because it is now a buyers' market.
- Wholesale real estate investing is a great entry for both new and seasoned investors because you can start today, you don't need much money or credit, you don't need previous experience, and you encounter significantly less risk than with other real estate investing strategies.

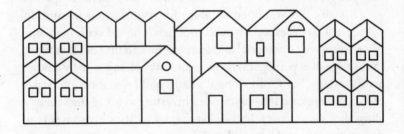

CHAPTER 2
The Truth About Wholesaling

Okay, be honest with me: You already had some negative thoughts about wholesale real estate before you picked up this book, right? Don't worry, I get it.

I don't take offense because traditional wholesale real estate has a bad reputation for a reason. Wholesaling can seem questionable because the barrier to entry is low, and there is so much miseducation on the internet, including on how you should conduct yourself in this type of transaction. This has led people to have misconceptions about what wholesaling is.

Here are the truths about wholesaling:
- Wholesaling is not predatory.
- Wholesaling is legal.
- Wholesaling is ethical.
- Wholesaling helps out homeowners when they need it most.

Wholesaling Is Not Predatory

One common assumption is that wholesale real estate is a predatory practice. The misconception is that we, as wholesalers, are taking advantage of people by lowballing unsophisticated homeowners, like grandmothers, out of their equity.

First, the types of properties that wholesalers should look for require significant repairs; or, in other words, some type of value-add or an opportunity to force appreciation. This means the equity we are supposedly stealing doesn't even exist without a significant financial risk by the homeowner. To be competitive, you must still pay top dollar for properties even in their distressed condition. Otherwise, you risk losing the opportunity to a higher offer. Your offer needs to reflect the home's current condition *and* its maximum potential. I never overpay, but I also don't lose out on an incredible opportunity.

To understand what that maximum value might look like, look for the gold-standard comparable. This means the nicest remodel with the best materials, meticulous attention to detail and design, and in a subdivision that has a lot to offer. This is your North Star comp to determine the maximum potential for this home. This is what wholesalers describe as the maximum amount after repair value (ARV), which informs the buyer of the potential that we're selling. A wholesaler's assignment fee is always paid by the buyer and always comes out of the buyer's potential profit (more on this in a later chapter). This is one area that has fueled ethical concerns in the wholesale real estate industry because there is no standard percentage to determine a fair assignment fee. For example, if a project has the potential to make a $50,000 profit for a fix-and-flip investor, is it fair for a wholesaler to make this equal amount? If you consider the different risks and resources, many people would say no. What critics don't realize, though, is that finding that deal may have cost the wholesaler $30,000 in marketing, months of sourcing new leads, and the time and effort of their entire team. The wholesaler's risk is entirely on the front end, whereas the buyer's is after they purchase the contract. So, that $50,000 profit for both the wholesaler and the investor looks a lot more reasonable after you understand the context of a wholesaler's business model.

Oftentimes, the properties that we buy are not financeable in their current condition. A traditional lender would require a significant investment to improve the property before a sale. Even making such improvements doesn't guarantee that the property will meet the standards of retail buyers. That top offer is similar to our ARV North Star, but it's not reflective of where the property is *today*.

Therefore, the individuals who are most likely to purchase an "as-is" home are buyers with the cash resources or those working with buyers who have cash resources. These are people who are comfortable taking on the risk of renovating and improving a property to its best value potential. Purchasing such distressed homes creates the most potential for the buyer and it significantly increases a wholesaler's likelihood of getting a higher assignment fee.

The lesson here is that when looking for properties, look for those with the largest potential difference between their as-is value and what you believe the max potential could be.

As a wholesaler, if you pay anything more than the as-is value for a home, then you're overpaying. Put on your businessperson hat to confirm that the costs you'll be paying upfront are reasonable. Remember, these opportunities for potential profit don't happen without the wholesaler putting in the risk on the front end.

Do you see now that wholesaling is not predatory because we pay 100 percent of the as-is value for the properties we contract? Our fees are paid by our buyers based on the property's potential. We don't steal the seller's equity because by the time the seller is ready to sell, the property has no equity left. That is frequently why the seller is selling.

Unfortunately, that's not the only misinformed issue people have with wholesalers.

Wholesaling Is Legal

Again, wholesaling is where you act as the principal in a transaction and sell your equitable interest to an investor who has the resources to force appreciation or create new potential in a property. One key legal element is your equitable interest.

Are equitable interest and equity the same thing? No.

Equitable interest is the interest that is held by an equitable title—that is, a title that indicates a beneficial interest in the property and gives the holder the right to acquire that legal title (this also includes interest claimed on equitable grounds, such as the interest held by a trust beneficiary). This means that wholesalers can buy a house through a standard purchase and sale agreement or through an option agreement (different types of agreements are discussed in a later chapter).

Equity, in its simplest terms, is the difference between how much a home is worth and how much the owner has left due on their mortgage. Equity and equitable interest are completely different terms, yet wholesalers have been accused of taking a home's equity when they are selling the equitable interest in a home.

Equitable interest only has value when there's potential in that property to be realized. A wholesaler's fee is not coming from the home's equity, but from selling the home's equitable interest. The bottom line is that wholesalers make their money from the potential of the property, not from the home's equity.

Wholesaling Is Ethical

The main ethical question is one of intent. If a wholesaler contracts a home they never intend to purchase but rather to resell to a third party, or doesn't have the resources to purchase, is their offer fraudulent? My answer is yes if the proper disclosures were not made to the seller. It's vitally important that before a wholesaler signs contracts and takes properties off the market, they or their buyers must have verifiable access to the cash resources needed to close the deal and have transparent disclosures in their contract to alert the homeowner of their intention, which is to sell their home and property to a third party (clauses to include in contracts are also discussed later in this book).

One important concept to clarify with all the parties is the fine line between wholesaling and brokering. A real estate broker is a professional responsible for managing transactions between buyers and sellers. I say outright that brokering without a real estate license is illegal. In a wholesale transaction, you are acting as the principal in the deal and are selling your rights to purchase the property to another buyer. In illegal brokering, you are not acting as the principal, you have no equitable interest, and you don't have a real estate license. Therefore, you have no legal right to collect any profits from the sale of the property.

It's understandable how people can get these two concepts confused. In a wholesale deal, the key difference is that the wholesaler is acting as the principal in the transaction and has the right to sell the home's equitable interest. These misunderstandings, and real predatory practices made by a small number of wholesalers, are why people believe that the entire industry is unethical. Not only is this untrue, but wholesaling can add tremendous value to communities and the real estate industry, can make neighborhoods safer, and more.

The positive cascade effect of a wholesaler begins when a distressed homeowner successfully sells their house for top dollar that would never sell on the retail market, as I explained in the Preface about the widower wanting to sell his home to move closer to his children. Or a rehabber gains a property they could not source themselves because they're busy managing their projects. Real estate agents are paid higher commissions by the sale at the highest dollar the house will get. Title companies are paid to facilitate the transactions, and contractors are paid to fix up the home or build new buildings on the property. Finally, the neighbors keep their home values because the sold property is bought by someone planning to improve the property.

Wholesalers Help Homeowners

When properties degrade to the point that banks won't finance them, a wholesaler may be the only resource a homeowner has to bring a buyer to the table. Plus, some sellers are more than happy to trade money for convenience. I have bought many homes from property owners who valued speed and ease over waiting for a higher price that was not coming.

Think of when you trade in a vehicle. You know that the dealer intends to make a profit on your trade-in. You could try to sell the vehicle yourself, but most of us are happy to hand over our keys, let the professionals do their jobs, and move on to our next car.

It was in the spirit of high ethics and solid legal principles that I started KeyGlee in 2016, along with my sister Rahima Blaza and with Josiah Grimes and Hunter Runyon. KeyGlee and our franchises have the financial backing to keep the promises we make to homeowners.

A wholesale franchise should be highly structured. Fundamentally, a franchise should be a "plug and play" system. This entails receiving the necessary tools, support, and infrastructure to go into business easily. A franchise offers you brand recognition without having to build one from scratch. In exchange for that recognition, you pay a royalty. (Note that every wholesale franchise structure is different, so do your homework.)

For example, KeyGlee has a unique approach to the wholesale business. We keep a focus on our relationships with real estate agents, other wholesalers, and those in the real estate industry. This allows our franchisees to forgo additional costs to find new leads. KeyGlee franchisees are supported by our corporate team, our acquisitions and dispositions support team,[1] and other franchisees, thanks to our

---

1 Disposition is the process of selling the equitable interest in a property that has been put under contract. It's also called wholesale disposition.

collaborative business format. We were recently recognized as one of the top 500 franchisers in the nation in *Entrepreneur* magazine.

You might be asking yourself at this point: How does a new investor, with no capital, ethically and legally wholesale?

Two words: Squad up. If you have no capital, you can partner with wholesaling firms or your cash buyers to ensure the contracts you enter into are fully backed by resources.

Next, only participate in deals where you hold an equitable interest. And approach every opportune transaction with honesty, so you can create win–win situations while becoming wealthy.

Now that true wholesaling has been defined versus what people think wholesaling is, it's time to dig into licensing and what that means as real estate investors and as wholesalers.

The next chapter talks about legislation and legitimacy, where wholesaling now stands in the industry, and how this could shape the future of wholesaling.

WHOLESALE SUCCESS STORY
Scaling Through Relationships with Helena Wu

I created my company, Abundance Real Estate, in September 2022 and started focusing on the Florida market. In October of that year, I did my first three deals back to back, all with the collaboration of wholesaling family members on the acquisitions or dispositions end. Between November 2022 and January 2023, that amount increased to four to five deals per month consistently. By May 2023, we are doing three to eight deals per week consistently, and if the properties are vacant, we can assign within twenty-four to forty-eight hours.

At this point, I am truly scaling effortlessly; I have buyers asking me for deals every day. I also have wholesalers and agents sending me deals as they know who I am, trust me, and love doing business with me because they know that I have their back as well. This constant and continuous growth is only possible because of the amazing relationships I have built with all these people. This concept of collaboration over competition was hard for me to understand at first, as this is not how I was brought up. But learning the power of collaboration from Jamil has been the key to success in my business.

Relationships are everything in this business and in life. This is how relationships have helped me to scale:

1. **Relationships with Wholesalers.** Initially, people who are more experienced in the community kindly helped me with feedback on my comping and underwriting, allowing me to understand numbers and master them. Most deals I have done are with other wholesalers. And having Jamil as a mentor in this community has been amazing—he leads by example, and he is patient and caring as he helps everyone to achieve success.

2. **Relationships with Your "Competitors."** Of the deals I do, 95 percent are through collaboration with other players in the market! For example, one of my biggest "competitors" in this market is also one of my biggest collaborators. We brainstorm how to build and grow the business, we share insights on the market, and we discuss market shifts. Not only are they a sounding board, they are an asset to my business—we have done so many deals together and are super close friends.

3. **Relationships with Your Team.** Building a team is indispensable for scaling. To run a good team, recognize the right talents and help them reach their full potential; this will bring out the best version of everyone and create a culture of appreciation. Hiring, retaining, and growing talent is key to scaling and success!

4. **Relationships with Agents, Wholesalers, and Buyers.** I have agents representing me, so they get more rewards on the deal. I also help wholesalers get their deals done while focusing on getting them paid and getting the seller paid. As a result, rewards come to me naturally. Finally, be sure to truly care about your buyer's interest. When you sell them a deal, ensure you bring value to them—that's the first priority, not how much you make from the deal. When you always focus on achieving everybody's best interests, you'll be better equipped to finesse what you want in life.

5. **Relationship with Yourself.** Be aware and brutally transparent with yourself about your daily inventory—how much

do you actually do every day? Fully accept who you are and where you are. Accept that you are at the exact right time and place for a reason. Also, give yourself grace. Love and encourage yourself like you would the person you love most in the world. Be connected with yourself, and listen to the guidance from your inner intuition. And finally, be courageous enough to, when necessary, depart from your old self to arrive at a better place.

6. **Relationship with God.** It has been super important for me to have a relationship with God, to understand that I am a part of something much bigger than myself. I believe that God brings everyone to the world for a purpose and that I am meant to be here and bring value to other people. This is God's intention and will.

Every single business involves more than one person—therefore, relationships are the nature of business. Take care of your relationships first, and they will take care of you. And remember, relationships are long-term things that require love, care, and patience. I have chosen many times to do a deal for free, just to help a seller solve their problem and move on with their life, to help agents get paid for their work, or to help buyers get the property they like. Is it worth it? Yes, absolutely. Every time! All relationship are seeds you plant—whether intentionally or unintentionally—and they will grow and come back to you.

A QUICK RECAP

- Wholesaling is not predatory because the goal is to pay top dollar for a property in its distressed condition. These properties require significant repairs, some type of value-add, or an opportunity to force appreciation.
- Wholesaling is legal because we are purchasing the equitable interest; that is, the right to buy a house through a standard purchase and sale agreement or through an option agreement. This is far different from illegal brokering.

- A wholesaler's fee does not come from the seller's equity but from selling the equitable interest of the property. Wholesalers make their money from the potential future value.
- Wholesaling is ethical because of our disclosure of intent to purchase the contract and then sell it to a qualified buyer.
- A wholesaler helps distressed homeowners by purchasing quickly at the home's as-is value and by providing solutions not available through an MLS listing.

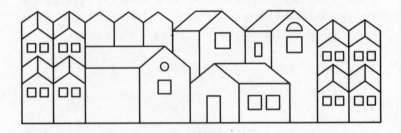

CHAPTER 3
Wholesaling Legislation and Licensing

As you've learned, wholesaling has had a bit of a dark past. Thankfully, there are people in the industry who are leading by example by being ethical wholesalers.

There will always be those bad apples. Sketchy wholesalers doing the wrong things. But recent laws and regulations are making it increasingly difficult to have unethical and unlawful behavior. The following takes a look at how these might impact wholesaling businesses (depending on your state or city licensing and what kind of wholesaler you want to be, meaning an acquisition or deposition wholesaler).

Wholesale Definition and State Legislation

In the previous chapter, I talked about the largest misconception that still remains: Is wholesaling legal? Real estate wholesaling is absolutely legal in every U.S. state. What I'll discuss in this chapter are the legalities and restrictions being placed on wholesalers in certain states.

Here are some examples of states that have recently changed their wholesale legislation:

- In Oklahoma, Illinois, and New York, you need to have a real estate license to wholesale.
- In Florida, you can assign contracts provided there is no language in the contract that prohibits wholesale, violates any public policies, or violates a state or federal statute.
- Philadelphia also requires a license, as well as paying a fee to the city of Philadelphia Department of Licenses and Inspections, offering specific disclosures, and adhering to a strict code of ethics.

Here is a visual representation of where wholesale is legal in the United States:

To repeat, wholesaling is legal in all fifty states, but it's important to keep in mind that while a state may not have any requirements or regulations, a particular city in that state might. Some might require additional disclosures in your contract or that you will take title (this is when you'll need transactional funding). These differences make it increasingly difficult to have standardized regulations; the laws vary depending on where you decide to practice wholesale real estate.

I'm often asked, "Why is legislation changing so much among the different states?" In my opinion, a lot of this centers on miseducation. The barrier to entry for wholesale is incredibly low, and it's gaining popularity as a strategy in the world of real estate investing. My first hypothesis is that there are clusters of influencers with large followings in certain geographical parts of the country, which has led to greater wholesale activities in those areas. Having so many new wholesalers who haven't been properly educated about how to wholesale legally and ethically in their area can lead to an increase in complaints. This inevitably leads to greater local media attention, which then leads to a push for state or federal legislation.

My second hypothesis is that areas with greater socioeconomic disparity have seen a significant increase in the number of wholesalers entering the field. For those already living in the area, it can provide a financial opportunity not otherwise available. With wholesale real estate being a low financial risk with high financial reward, it is an attractive occupation to pursue.

My third hypothesis involves the National Association of Realtors® fielding complaints from real estate agents who have lost business to wholesale activity or have had clients who have been damaged by wholesalers who operated unethically or illegally. This has pushed the NAR to support wholesaling legislation specifically aimed at metro areas that have greater concentrations of NAR agents.

The NAR is also at the forefront of pushing for wholesale licensing and regulations. The NAR's argument is that wholesaling is no different from what a real estate agent does because wholesalers are sourcing deals for buyers. Standard licensing law states that if you're not the principal in the transaction, then you must have a license; so to the NAR, wholesale deals should be no different. The NAR would like additional regulations because they don't like factors such as:

- A wholesaler can assign their contract with the seller to another buyer using an assignment contract (all contract types are discussed later in the book).

- A wholesaler doesn't directly have the money to purchase a property, but is looking for a buyer, making their offers seem fraudulent.
- Many wholesalers use non-NAR-approved purchase and sale contracts, allowing for loopholes and escape hatches not regularly seen in standard real estate transactions.

Let me start by saying that I agree with the NAR wanting to create standardization regulation across the industry. I'm one of the few wholesalers who do. But I think it's important to note again the misconceptions and stereotypes laid out in earlier chapters. If and when the opportunity for standardization comes, I hope that we're able to discuss regulations that truly protect consumers and aren't based on a narrative of fear and outdated misconceptions. Let's dispel some of them now.

From the NAR's perspective, anyone connecting a buyer and seller needs to have a license. I agree with that. However, in a wholesale deal, wholesalers are the principal, so we do own the rights to purchase a property on our own behalf. Wholesalers do not directly connect a buyer and seller. Any conversations between a contract holder and a potential buyer regarding the purchase of their contract should be confidential and protected, as they are in any other legal transaction.

Related to NAR's legality concerns, it's all about intent. I agree that it is illegal and deceptive to put a house under contract with no stated intention to purchase it for resale or without access to the funds needed to purchase it. Brokering is the term used in much of the legislation, but politicians and the NAR incorrectly assume this is what wholesalers are doing. This type of assumption, especially from a highly regarded regulatory body like the NAR, can lead to labeling the industry as a whole as fraudulent and illegal, which is not correct. The best way to ensure that the wholesaling industry thrives with ethics is to create a well-educated regulatory body with a standardized code of ethics and practices, and to hold all wholesalers accountable to them. I've discussed this topic several times in podcasts and interviews, and have gotten some hate mail in return, but I do believe that regulation would be helpful.

Here's an example of a controversy that led to legislation that I disagree helps protect the public. In 2021, FM radio station WABE in Atlanta, Georgia, did a four-part series called "Equity Theft," investigating complaints from homeowners in Atlanta who felt they were the victims of predatory practices and commercial harassment from wholesalers. The resulting municipal regulation prohibits predatory tactics in the city, which are defined as "repeated and unsolicited attempts, within any 180-day period, to contact a person or entity including via personal visits, or written material or similar means . . . where the person or entity has affirmatively requested the defendant or the defendant's agent to refrain from such activity." In some of these reported cases, the wholesalers were using common marketing techniques used by Fortune 500 companies, such as direct mail, billboard advertising, and door-knocking campaigns. The regulation frames the homeowners as feeling that these tactics created additional pressure on them to sell their properties. This could be true. But then again, marketing's purpose is to create pressure to sell or buy something. For example, like many of us, I receive letters announcing preapproval for credit cards that I don't need or want. For some who need access to extra credit, all of those letters will have paid off. Every day, we're inundated with online ads for products designed to be impulse purchases. Every day we're influenced by a franchise restaurant billboard on where to have lunch. Is it fair to label these examples as commercial harassment?

I note here that in this case, the ordinance was specifically applied to the city of Atlanta, not to the entire state of Georgia. That is why it's essential for wholesalers to know both their local regulations and their state's regulations.

Wholesaling Standardization and Licensing

Clearly, after describing the ethical concerns facing wholesalers and the new legislation in Atlanta pushed by the NAR, I'm on board with having some standardization when it comes to wholesaling, but it must be appropriate. For example, I don't believe that a real estate license should be *legally* required, yet I believe that wholesalers should have their real estate license. This legitimizes you and your business, gives you access to better tools, and opens a host of networking opportunities. While I admit to not having one, every KeyGlee staff person has their license, which mean I'm always working with a licensed person.

Holding a real estate license gives you the foundational credibility to earn trust quickly from prospects. It allows a consumer to quickly vet that you've met the minimum requirements needed to represent them in a transaction. Licensing provides you with an understanding of the laws in your local area and state and ensures that you're operating in compliance. I believe there's a lot missing from the licensing process, like requiring real estate agents to learn how to comp properties, yet it's still a good place to start establishing your legitimacy as a real estate professional.

You will also want a foundation in the software and tools you will use in your day-to-day activities. Oftentimes, unlicensed wholesalers are forced to use third-party tools for seller information, pricing information, comping, and more; yet these tools may not have the most accurate data. With a real estate license (or working with agents who have licenses), you'll have access to real-time data tools, such as the MLS.

Being a licensed real estate agent also allows you to connect easier with other real estate agents, who tend to give more respect to those who also hold a license. These relationships are a crucial component that connects you with investors, buyers, and sellers. I'll go more in depth on these relationships in an upcoming chapter.

Having a license can open doors, but there are definite challenges to obtaining one. For instance, it takes time and is costly. Here in Arizona, the online course to get prelicensing is between $400 and $600 and takes ninety hours to complete. It costs $135 to take the exam, and there's a $67 charge for a fingerprint clearance card. If you want to become a member of NAR, that's an additional $150 per year, but that is an optional cost. Keep in mind that each state has its own requirements and costs; for example, Colorado requires 168 hours of prelicense education but Alabama lets you off with sixty hours.

One misconception keeping some people from getting their

license is that it will prevent them from working as a wholesale agent. It was this misconception that kept me from obtaining my own license. Nevertheless, over the many years and thousands of deals that I've completed, I've met hundreds of licensed real estate agents who are successful wholesalers. You can absolutely be a wholesaler and hold a real estate license. With this license, you disclose your intent and know the clearly defined obligations and limitations. Because I have always been the principal in transactions, I never thought it necessary decades later to obtain my real estate license. However, when I formed KeyGlee, I knew that my employees would be acting on my behalf and not as true principals. That is why my employees must be licensed.

If we could have standardized practices for wholesalers, it would keep those working in the field honest and help with the public's perceptions. I would be the first in line to obtain this license, but only when there is agreement on what that should include.

In the early part of 2022, I sat down with Jerry Norton, Brent Daniels, and Pace Morby, three of wholesale's prominent industry leaders. We not only discussed what's happening in the industry but also how we could possibly start the process of a unified licensing protocol. The outcome was the creation of a 501(c)(6) nonprofit organization called the National Real Estate Wholesalers Association, which encourages and empowers wholesalers, most of whom don't have a voice in our current political system. Having an association like this will give real estate wholesalers a presence and offer the opportunity to create a standardized code of ethics to which we can be held accountable. The more we can show how we work ethically and professionally within the community and the industry as a whole, the better our reputation among consumers and regulatory bodies like NAR.

This chapters deals with regulations and other consequential information, and stresses that you should check your local and state ordinances. Next, I'll show how to build a wholesale business, starting with making sure that your mindset is in the right place.

A QUICK RECAP

- Know the local and state laws where you want to do business.
- Legislation and regulations within the industry are being pushed by the NAR and various consumer protection agencies due to years of misinformation and miscommunication about the wholesale real estate sector.
- There should be checks and balances within the industry, but without restricting the solutions that wholesalers provide to homeowners. The new National Real Estate Wholesalers Association hopes to provide a political voice for wholesalers.

SECTION II
Building Up Your Wholesale Business

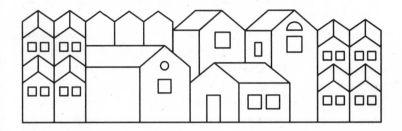

CHAPTER 4
Creating a Successful Mindset

In the previous section, we talked about what wholesale real estate is, misconceptions in the sector, and how regulations differ among cities and states. Understanding the foundation and history of wholesaling gives you the framework under which you can start building your ethical wholesale real estate business. Whether you're in wholesale or fix-and-flip real estate, your success has everything to do with your mindset.

I can honestly say the most successful wholesalers that I know have common and overlapping beliefs about how important their thinking and belief system are to their success. As a coach to new wholesalers, I have seen for myself that there is a strong correlation between having a good mindset and having phenomenal results. Notice that I said good mindset, not phenomenal mindset, because it's important to understand that you need to do only a little bit of work on yourself to have disproportionately positive results.

What's Your Mindset?

As I mentioned earlier in the book, I lost millions of dollars in the 2008 recession and I was financially at my worst. My life had gotten so bad that I was drinking every day, felt completely disconnected from my family, and lost touch with my own purpose. I became numb to everything.

It took my wife getting severely sick and needing medication costing $6,000 that we couldn't afford that pulled me out of my haze to look for solutions outside of a liquor bottle. I had two choices: rob a pharmacy or make $6,000 in less than a week. I chose the latter, of course. I went back to real estate, and I spent days scouring Facebook for cash buyers. I put together a wholesale transaction that would close fast enough for me to get the money I needed to save my wife's life.

Even after pulling off a lifesaving miracle, I was still a mess and knew I needed help. I found myself in the self-help section at Barnes & Noble (there's nothing like the smell of Starbucks and a good book to reevaluate your life), and I felt guided to the book *You Are a Badass* by Jen Sincero. Inside, she spoke about how every successful person she ever met meditated regularly. She didn't understand how or why it worked, but rich people meditated.

I thought, "Heck, what do I have to lose? I've got nothing else going on right now." I desperately needed some positivity, and if sitting quietly for a few minutes a day could get me there, I'd give it a try. After reading her book, I woke up one morning (with a hangover), downloaded an app called Headspace, and began my journey to the inside of myself. When I redirected my energy using meditation and visualization to align with the purpose I had lost sight of, my life changed.

I can tell you that everything we experience is energy. The law of conservation of energy states that energy can neither be created nor destroyed; it can only be transformed or transferred from one form to another. What a gift! Now, all your energy needs to go somewhere, and that's into your actions and decisions. For me, the law of attraction and manifestation comes down to human beings converting their potential energy of thought into their physical reality.

While many of you may think I've gone off on an unrelated tangent, these principles are rooted in centuries of scientific observation. For me, within a few months, the desire to drink every day disappeared. After one particular meditation session, an idea came to me to build a wholesale company that was nationally branded and would help wholesalers across the country. The problem I kept seeing was wholesalers canceling contracts, and there were a lot of cancellations. I realized that it wasn't because the deals weren't good; it was because when a wholesaler, for example, specialized in acquisitions, they spent their time focused on lead generation. They didn't focus on talking to buyers, so when they did secure a property, they had no one to sell it to. And thus the deal fell through.

I saw an opportunity to build relationships with cash buyers at scale and provide a disposition service to wholesalers to reduce the number of deals that fell through at the last minute. I shopped that idea around in Phoenix, and everyone in real estate turned me down. They said I was too ambitious, that I needed to stay in my own lane, and that my idea would never work. They were absolutely wrong. If I had listened to them, I would have never formed KeyGlee, touched thousands of lives for the better, and I wouldn't have written this book.

My business insights and the compass that guides my decision-making comes from routinely meditating and visualizing what I want to accomplish in a day, a quarter, a year, or in five years. This small yet not-so-small change to my thinking and routine pulled me out of rock bottom and helped me to build a thriving wholesale franchise business.

This evolution of thinking heavily informs my perspective when I'm teaching. Experiences that have happened in your life (including those happening now) have a profound impact your mindset. If you don't take the time to think about these or become aware of your preconceptions, they can negatively impact on your business before you even begin. These thoughts can prevent you from achieving your goals and reaching your full potential. We may feel greed and push ourselves just to make more money. We may experience jealousy over what others have. We may feel discouraged because we think we don't have the ability to change, or something is too hard. For me, the burden of past mistakes was stopping me from providing for my family.

As a mentor, the most common limiting belief that I see is on the issue of self-worth. So many people who have the potential to be incredibly successful in this business aren't because they don't believe that they could be. When we hear that someone makes a million dollars in a day, in a week, in a month, it shocks us. It doesn't compute. How can someone who has the same twenty-four hours in a day make millions of dollars while I sink further into debt? There are a lot of reasons why that might be the case—poor socioeconomic conditions, no financial support, no established network—but one factor that we can control is our mindset. When was the last time you told yourself you could make a million dollars in a week? If you said never, then maybe it's time to start thinking that you could.

Read that again. It is possible for you to make a million dollars in a week. If that statement makes you uncomfortable, that's good! Congrats—you've just identified a limiting belief that's currently in your mind right now. Okay, maybe you don't start out making a million dollars a week; maybe it's just $1,000, or perhaps it's $6,000 for your wife's medication. But if you don't believe that you have the potential to succeed, you won't.

I know you weren't expecting homework, but I'd like you to do an exercise before you continue reading. I want you to list your mental limits that already exist related to your financial potential. Really consider your answers to these questions:

- How much money is too much money?
- How much money would give you financial freedom?
- How much money would it take for you to be living your best life?
- What do you think is necessary in order to achieve it?
- Do you believe that you can?

I didn't believe that I could do it for a long time, and quite frankly I didn't want to. I had the skills, I had the drive, I had the experience, but I let my mindset stop me from using the tools I already had to achieve my fullest potential. I told you at the beginning of this book that I made many mistakes along my journey. Don't let this be one of yours.

Another lie that we tell ourselves is that to make money, we must do something wrong. We think the only people who get far in life are those who screw others over. As a society, we believe that the most successful people also have the most compromised ethics. Take, for example, Elizabeth Holmes, the disgraced creator of Theranos. She misled high-profile investors to the tune of millions of dollars. She knowingly misdiagnosed her patients. Before her downfall, Holmes was widely praised for her groundbreaking innovations, and now she's a cautionary tale about manipulation and greed.

I'm here to tell you that the notion of having to be unethical to achieve unimaginable success is totally untrue. I've built businesses structured on ethics and empathy. Everything my team does stems from having high levels of integrity and moral character. We want to give people the opportunity to be successful, believe in their potential for that success, and feel proud to achieve it in an ethical manner. You can build your business on the same ethical foundation. But first, you must believe that you deserve the level of success that you're capable of achieving.

I've been in deals where I sold land to a national homebuilder. They paid my company millions of dollars on this one project. Some people might say that what I was paid was unethical only because they presume that I could not have done the deal without being shady. The truth is that my success, and your success, is based on conducting business with ethical practices and providing significant potential value to the other parties involved. This all comes back to the misconceptions about wholesale and how people often view the industry as predatory or manipulative. Any massive financial gains must be tainted. I say that to be a successful wholesaler, you can't fall prey to crude misconceptions. You must believe that you will be an ethical wholesaler and that you deserve all the financial compensation for the effort that you put into a deal.

This type of thinking doesn't just apply to business-to-business transactions; it can apply to friends, family, and colleagues as well. Have you ever expected a discount on a product or service just because a friend owned the business? Why? Have you ever felt compelled to give a discount on your services just because a family member was asking? Why? It gives you a glimpse into your subconscious beliefs about money. You don't have to compromise to be successful in business. You do have to shift your mindset to focus on what your decisions mean for your bottom line. You are providing value for your services, and you deserve fair compensation for that. Your services are not related to the time it takes you to complete the deal but to the amount of value you provide and the skills it took for you to provide it. Time is unrelated to the value you bring. The value is the same whether you spent one day or one month on the project.

It is worth your time to examine these personal beliefs before starting a business because if your relationship with money and success is unhealthy, then you're sabotaging your potential before you've even started. Surprise: More homework! Ask yourself these questions:

- What does it mean to you to run a business ethically?
- Do you feel that you have to compromise your ethical boundaries to achieve the highest level of success?
- How much money is it okay to make if you're doing a deal with family or friends?
- Do you feel bad charging friends or family for a service?
- Do you believe that you deserve success?

Your answers to these questions will tell you about your relationship with money and what you need to examine before handling the finances of an entire business. If you can't charge your friends for your services without feeling bad, or can't think about earning a six-figure payday without feeling like an unethical person, those are limiting beliefs worth examining before you ever close your first deal.

If you want to practice improving your mindset or quieting negative statements, check out Matthew Ferry's fantastic book *Quiet Mind Epic Life: Escape the Status Quo & Experience Enlightened Prosperity Now*. He's an author, speaker, and spiritual teacher, and I swear I'm not getting residuals from him. His book is simply too good to not share.

A QUICK RECAP

- Having a good mindset is crucial to succeeding in both business and in life.
- Limiting beliefs such as not believing in your ability to be successful or believing that making a lot of money means you have to be unethical will prevent you from achieving your true potential.
- Sit down and dive deep into your homework answers to understand how your mindset and beliefs are limiting your potential for success.

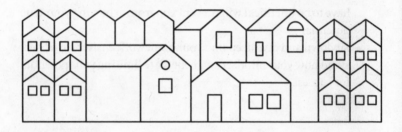

CHAPTER 5
Mission Acquisition

Now that we've gone over the fundamentals of wholesaling and you've learned about incorporating the right mindset for business, you're at the point to start learning how to get your first deal. Yay! This portion of the wholesale process is better known as acquisitions, which is the process of gaining ownership or control of real property that has some type of distress or potential to add or create new value. As mentioned in earlier chapters, these types of properties or situations are ideal for wholesalers because they often have the most potential for forced appreciation.

Property distress is easy to spot because it's often visual from the outside, such as property with overgrown lawns, mail piling up, and broken windows. Worse, there may be squatters living in the abandoned home. With these telling signs of deferred maintenance on the property, it's easy to explain to a seller that significant investment is required to get it to future potential. The seller most likely just wants out, and the neighbors want to get rid of the eyesore pulling down their property taxes.

There are two types to know about: distressed property and distressed situations.

DISTRESSED PROPERTY

These normally require a significant investment to bring the property back to retail standard. The greatest opportunities are oftentimes found in these properties because the sellers don't have the financial resources required to fix their property, so there's limited to no chance for them to increase the home's value or reach a habitable standard. Here are other signs to look for once you do some research: The property may be antiquated or outdated, it may be uninhabitable, or there may be city and/or homeowner association (HOA) violations. These types of distress can be found through research in city records, violation lists, HOA companies, court actions, or any additional issue placed on a property. Most of these resources should be a matter of public record, so you don't need to go through the homeowner in order to secure them.

Data aggregating technology resources have also made it easy for investors to find lists of properties that have one or more indicators of distress. My favorite websites to use are Privy and BatchLeads because they are relatively inexpensive and have current, accurate information. These platforms allow you to create lists, comp properties, skip trace phone numbers (that is, using a property's known address to find the owner), and manage contacts. I use these online resources to find most of my deals, although there are other options I'll explain in this chapter. What's also helpful is that you do not need a real estate license to use these resources, which is unlike the MLS that does require proof of a license to use.

DISTRESSED SITUATION

These may not be as easy to identify because they are situations that require a homeowner to sell their property faster than the traditional sale cycle. Think of the example of the widower with the custom mansion I mentioned in the Preface.

Distressed situations include:
- Foreclosures.

- Delinquent tax bills.
- HOA liens.
- Mechanic liens.
- Judgments.
- Relocations.
- Probate.
- Medical bills.

Let's dive a bit deeper into these situations.

FORECLOSURES

A foreclosure happens when a homeowner falls behind on their loan or mortgage payments. While one or two missed payments aren't legal cause for a foreclosure, the home is at risk once payments have lapsed past the ninety-day period. Foreclosure is still possible regardless of repayment plans or other financial options offered to the homeowner. The specifics of the process vary from state to state, and even city to city, but the general process begins when the lender files a notice of default and notifies the homeowner how much time they have to rectify the situation. If the homeowner cannot meet the timeframe, the lender obtains a court order, or a trustee may initiate this process, to sell the property to recoup the balance. The property can be sent to auction to be sold or becomes the property of the lender to do with as they choose.

A wholesaler would want to intervene when a home is in pre-foreclosure, and lists of these homes are available on platforms like BatchLeads. In the pre-foreclosure process, wholesalers offer the homeowner a fair cash price and close on the property prior to the foreclosure date. Under the right circumstances, this might allow the homeowner to pay off their missing loan balance, including the arrears, fines, or penalties that have accrued, and also get much-needed cash in their hands. Some factors that could affect this outcome include the total balance owed on the house, the timeframe of the foreclosure action, and the type of debt the homeowner is liable for (e.g., other liens such as for medical bills).

DELINQUENT TAX BILLS

When a homeowner fails to pay their property tax bill, the taxing authority, whether that's a county or municipality, can take steps to collect the unpaid taxes. This can include adding extra fees or penalties to the bill or starting a legal action (e.g., selling the home or property at a tax sale). A wholesaler can obtain a list of homes that are behind on tax payments. Conversations with these homeowners may reveal opportunities to purchase the property, especially if owning the property poses financial or personal burdens for the owner.

HOA LIENS

HOA liens happen when owners stop paying their fees and assessments. The allows the HOA to start a lien foreclosure, which allows the association to sell the property in order to recover the unpaid fees. It's similar to a standard foreclosure, but the HOA has more limited reach in its legal recourse because it is not a financial institution holding a debt securitized against the property. A wholesaler who obtains a list of properties with HOA liens could cold-call the homeowners to discover if there's a financial hardship that could be solved by the sale of the property.

MECHANIC LIENS

A mechanic lien is a legal claim against a property that's been filed by a contractor, subcontractor, or supplier for unpaid goods or services. This might be unpaid renovation expenses, delinquent product invoices, or outstanding labor liabilities. The process for a mechanic lien starts when a contractor provides notice to the property owner that they intend to file a lien to retrieve overdue payments on their products or services. A mechanic lien must be submitted within a specific time period after the services are rendered. As with all other things, that time period varies from state to state. As with an HOA lien, if a homeowner does not pay off this debt, the property might end up with a lien foreclosure. Wholesalers can obtain a list of these liens to investigate if the sale of the property could resolve the homeowner's distressed situation.

JUDGMENTS

A judgment lien is a court ruling that gives a creditor the right to take possession of a debtor's property if the debtor fails to fulfill their contractual obligations. These liens can be attached to real or personal property. If a debtor doesn't currently own property, these judgments can be applied to any future acquisitions. Wholesalers can also obtain a list of these liens and talk to the owners. You might be the answer to their financial problems.

RELOCATIONS

Relocations are often thought of as a form of moving, but they're a bit different. Rather than moving from one suburb to another one nearby, relocations involve people moving across cities or states. Relocations mainly happen due to changes in employment, and there was a noticeable uptick during and in the aftermath of the COVID-19 pandemic. With the job market being in tumult, many people changed jobs, lost jobs, were able to work remotely, or moved to be closer to family. There are real estate agents who specialize in relocations, and I suggest that you form relationships with them as a great lead source for potential acquisitions. You can also form relationships with corporate relocation companies to provide their clients an easy cash solution, especially when the relocation is happening in a compressed timeframe.

PROBATE

Probate is a legal process that occurs after a property owner has passed away. A court first validates the deceased person's will, after which their assets are distributed according to the will. In some cases, this means resolving outstanding debts or taxes owed by the deceased property owner, which is usually handled by the executor of the will. This may lead to the sale of the home either by the court or the beneficiaries named in the will to generate the cash needed to cover these costs. As with the other types of situations discussed here, a wholesaler can obtain a list of properties that have entered the probate process. I recommend the website www.alltheleads.com. It's important to note that extra sensitivity is required when dealing with probate situations. The estate's representative is often a close relative and is likely going through the grieving process while also handling their loved one's personal and financial affairs.

MEDICAL BILLS

Remember my need for $6,000 to save my wife's life? Health care in America is exorbitantly expensive. If you've ever gotten a hospital bill, then you know how expensive they can get, even when you're only in a room for twenty-four hours. Unfortunately, many people must stay longer, which is far more costly. How can someone pay off a hospital stay, perhaps need rehab and ongoing medication, while at home utility and tax bills pile up? In 2019, one in ten adults in the United States had medical debt, with a grand total of $195 billion owed.

These distressed situations may cause a homeowner to look for financial assistance, such as selling their home or property on the traditional market. While this might provide the cash needed to cover their bills, this isn't necessarily a quick solution. Again, think of the widower in the Preface, who sat with his property for nine months without an offer. A wholesaler can provide a faster solution and give a homeowner the much-needed cash injection to help pay their bills and get out of debt.

Wholesalers Can Help Those in Distressed Situations

On average, when a seller lists—and this is assuming the property is in top retail condition—a property can take up to ninety days to go under contract and then another forty-five to sixty days to close. This doesn't include negotiations—or worse, cancellations and financing falling apart. A cash offer can be an attractive option because it often allows you and the homeowner to avoid the pitfalls of a natural property sale cycle.

In 2016, I was approached by a couple who was facing both foreclosure and a divorce. While the divorce was amicable, both parties were in desperate need of funds that were trapped in the home. Because of everything else they had going on, the homeowners hadn't taken any actions to rectify their foreclosure situation. With an auction just days away, they called me. How did they get my number? It was given to them by a real estate agent who had previously used my expertise to help out another client with a cash solution. This is why you want to have working relationships and networks with all types of real estate agents.

The homeowners faced several challenges. For one, because of the impending auction, there was no time to list the home on the MLS. For another, if the property went to auction, most—if not all—of the home's equity would've been lost to penalties, interest, auction fees, and the underlying mortgage. Essentially, if these homeowners couldn't get a deal in time, they would be left with nothing.

Now, the property itself was in serious disrepair, but it was in an up-and-coming neighborhood. Plus, I already had buyer relationships in the area. A cash offer was the only appropriate solution for the timeframe. I wholesaled the contract as an exit strategy to put all the pieces together. This transaction allowed the homeowners to walk away with $40,000 cash and stay in the home for an additional ninety days. This relieved their pressure of having to pack up everything and find two places to live immediately.

As a wholesaler with experience in the area, I was able to help the sellers negotiate favorable terms and timelines. At this point, even their real estate agent wasn't interested in continuing with the seller because there was no longer any opportunity to make a commission. However, I saw an opportunity to help these two people. Plus, I received an assignment fee of $10,000 by selling the contract to a rehabber, who now had a new property to fix and sell. The homeowners felt I was owed far more because I helped them so dramatically just days before an auction. I received such a heartfelt thank-you that the card remains on my mantle at home.

LIST PROVIDERS

Data aggregators, also known as list providers, are companies that specialize in providing comprehensive national real estate data, such as distressed situation or property lists, mortgage information, vacancy status, tax and payment information, as well as ownership contact information. Using a list provider can speed things up. First, it can give you the information you need in one place to find out about the seller, allowing you to tailor your conversation to address their specific situation. You can create a profile of the person so you know who you're talking to and how to best approach and handle the conversation. Many of the homeowners you'll be speaking to are in distressed situations and deeply worried about the future of their family and their living situation. That's why you always want to be sympathetic to their situation. You want to enter the conversation as someone trying to help solve their pain point, not create a new one.

Second, list providers save you time and make you more efficient. You could chase the information you need yourself, but it won't be as accurate or as fast. List providers are experts at data gathering, and they know what information we need. The SMS platform my office prefers is BatchLeads because it allows you to send SMS blasts to large audiences while remaining compliant with the Telephone Consumer Protection Act (TCPA) (SMS blasts are discussed further in Chapter 8).

THE TCPA

Why do we need to stay compliant with the TCPA? It's because the TCPA regulates telemarketing calls, auto-dialed calls, prerecorded calls, text messages, and unsolicited faxes. It is the authority behind the National Do Not Call list. The Federal Communications Commission created and monitors the TCPA to protect people from getting inundated with telemarketing calls. You've gotten them, I've gotten them, and they can be extremely annoying. Now, this does not mean that wholesalers cannot cold-call people. It does mean that we must observe TCPA guidelines. BatchLeads makes sure that you stay within those guidelines. Having a texting or calling script makes it easier to outline what you want to tell a seller, follow compliance rules, and boost your confidence because you have a tried-and-true method to follow.

Two Types of Acquisition Techniques

As you've learned, wholesale acquisitions is the process of gaining ownership or control of real property that has upside potential. As I noted earlier in the book, many people are confused about wholesaling because they think they must buy the house or property outright. And while that could be true, this is rarely the case. In most wholesale transactions, you only contract for the *right* to purchase the home or property at a negotiated and agreed-upon price and terms. You then sell that right to the true buyer/investor/principal. This is made clear in the chapter on the types of contracts used in wholesaling.

There are two main strategies to wholesale acquisition to know about. These are:

- Transactional.
- Relational.

While both of these are valid strategies, one requires constant financial input to function, and the other builds a more sustainable, consistent, and free lead flow.

TRANSACTIONAL APPROACH

The transactional strategy is based on personal interactions that revolve around cost and benefit. Individuals are incentivized both to get and give as much as they can in the relationship. The most common form of a transactional strategy is direct-to-seller marketing; this means the investor is working directly with the seller of real property to negotiate a deal. There are six distinct types of direct-to-seller marketing:

1. Pay-per-click.
2. Cold calling.
3. Direct mail.
4. Bandit signs.
5. TV and radio ads.
6. Door knocking/Driving for dollars.

The following sections explain these six types.

Pay-Per-Click

Pay-per-click, or PPC, advertising is where an investor pays online providers (e.g., search engines) to find potential sellers, also called leads. No doubt you've seen these types of ads. They come in all shapes and sizes, usually with text, images, and videos. They'll typically include wording such as "Sell your house for cash!" or "We buy houses!"

The key performance indicators (KPIs) for PPC vary significantly depending on the digital marketing agency you're using and their ability to convert traffic. My friend R.J. Bates is a heavy user of PPC for his wholesale business. He shared with me the following KPIs that he uses to measure performance:

- Average cost per exclusive lead = $500.
  - An exclusive means that this lead is assigned to only your company.
- Seven leads cost per contract
  - Average cost per contract = $3,500.
  - Cost depends on area, so low-appreciation/low-demand areas might be lower in cost than high-appreciation/high-demand areas.

Cold Calling

Cold calling involves obtaining a list of potential prospects with contact information from manual research of public databases or for purchase from data aggregating list providers who consolidate that information for you. Some examples of data aggregating companies are BatchService, Privy, and PropStream. Wholesalers then call thousands of these people in hopes of finding someone who is interested in selling their property quickly. The success of cold calling is directly related to the list that's used, the number of phone calls made, and the skill level of the acquisition wholesaler. There are many companies that specialize in selling filtered lists of homeowners who might be experiencing certain types of distress, making this process more targeted but also more cost intensive. One great benefit of cold calling is its proactive approach; the greater your effort, the greater your results.

According to Brent Daniels, a cold-calling coach, it's important to keep the following KPIs in mind.[2] These metrics are reflective of an average salesperson's performance:

- Average cost per contract if calling yourself = ~ $1,000 (for list and skip tracing).
- Average cost per contract using acquisition manager = ~ $8,200 (for 3 months of pay + list. Based off $600/week draw for 90 days + lead list).
- Average number of conversations to reach 1 deal = 200 (distressed list).
  - 10% (~ 20 people) will consider an offer.
  - One person will transact in the next 90 days.
- Number of follow-up actions required to win a contract = 8 to 16 per seller.
- Number of days to get 1 deal (talking to 20 homeowners per day) = ~ 90 days.

The quality of your conversations will of course greatly impact your ability to convert deals. Confidence, tone of voice, and negotiation style will vary from wholesaler to wholesaler or to your team members. Chapter 9 includes cold-calling scripts and information on how to convert a lead into a contract.

Direct Mail

One of the oldest forms of marketing to sellers is direct mail. This is often referred to as the "dinosaur approach" because these mailers typically end up dead in the recycling bin. More and more people are requesting to be taken off these types of solicitation lists because of their general annoyance with this type of marketing and the growing push for environmental consciousness. Nevertheless, direct mail can still be quite lucrative in certain markets, with particular demographics, and related to property types. For example, I find direct mail to be a more respectful form of communication for families who have recently suffered the loss of a loved one and entered the probate

---

2   To learn more about Brent Daniels's expert cold-calling techniques for wholesalers, visit www.wholesalinginc.com/.

process. I don't use cold calling in these cases.

Hundreds of investors continue to use direct mail in some form, depending on region and population. The typical cost per contract ranges from $3,000 to $10,000. There are several direct mail options, but the two most common types used in real estate are postcards and yellow/personal letter.

Postcard

Many wholesalers prefer postcards because they are much cheaper than a yellow letter. Some of the headlines used to capture people's attention are "Final Notice" and "Warning," which are designed to elicit fearful reactions from recipients. This messaging has an initial shock value but the back-end returns tend to be quite low. A few standard points these mailers tend to include are:

- All cash offer.
- Quick close.
- No agents.
- No showings.
- No repairs required.
- As-is sale.

THIRD NOTICE

Attention: I have been trying to reach you regarding your property.

I'm hoping that this card catches you in time. I've tried for hours to find your phone number using the Internet but was unable to. : (

I've recorded a brief message about your property so that you could at least hear me out, then decide if we should speak over the phone.

All you have to do is **call 555-123-4567 to listen to my recorded message about this matter.** Call 24 hours a day, 7 days a week to listen to my message. **(No one will answer.)**

I would appreciate you keeping this matter private.

There are a few outcomes that a postcard may produce. Some people may ignore the postcard and toss it into their recycle bins, while others may be annoyed about the environmental impact. It might make people worried or fearful—and eventually angry—when they realize it's just a mailer. Worse, if you make fraudulent claims, it could scare someone into thinking they need to sell their home when that's not the case. Some people will hang onto these mailers to contact you at a later date. These sellers may be thinking about a future relocation. Or they worry about their inability to rectify a current distressed situation. As already mentioned, direct mail can be very expensive and can take time before you see results. On average, you can expect a 1 percent to 2 percent response rate, so if you're using postcard direct mail, you'll need a sizeable budget and enough time to run your campaign, sending postcards every other month for up to six months. Your prospect usually requires two to three pieces of mail before they call you.

Yellow/Personal Letter

A yellow/personal letter mailer is meant to look nearly indistinguishable from real mail. They tend to come in envelopes with realistic-looking handwriting and a personalized message. The goal is to get you to open and read it right away. Because of the customized medium, these tend to be more expensive than postcards. There's the cost of the envelopes, paper, printing, postage, etc. There also might be a cost to fold the letter—yes, this is a real thing—not to mention the time involved in sending it out to each individual on your list. Because it looks like important mail, there's a higher response rate for this type of direct mail. It isn't immediately noticeable as a typical mailer, so most people will open it, and then more people will call. It's personalized, so it feels more important. If you're like me, you open mail that arrives in an envelope. Meanwhile, all the other obvious mailers are immediately thrown into the recycling bin.

It isn't just the type of mailer you send that can impact the likelihood of a response; it also depends on the list of people you send it to. Here are some of the typical ideal prospects:

- Absentee owners.

- Pre-foreclosure.
- Inherited/Probate.
- City violation.
- Landlord list.
- Vacant and/or condemned properties.
- Tired landlord.
- Empty nester.
- High equity.

One thing to keep in mind about direct mail is election cycles, which may differ by state, city, and even jurisdiction, because these cycles can greatly affect the cost and effectiveness of direct mail campaigns. Wholesalers will suspend mail campaigns leading up to and during elections. The average response rate for personal letter direct mail campaigns is 3 percent to 5 percent, so you need the budget and time to complete your process.

Another thing to consider is that direct mail can be substantially more or less effective depending on your chosen market. For example, direct mail works well in low-appreciation/low-demand markets like Birmingham, Alabama. In highly competitive markets, like Phoenix, Arizona, you are likely to see a lower response rate.

Bandit Signs

Aptly named for their (il)legality, bandit signs are a guerrilla marketer's best friend. You've seen these because they are on every corner of busy intersections or are stapled high on telephone poles. Bandit signs are cheap and loud, which is why politicians use them. These signs can cost as little as $1 to produce, which can get you a lot of eyeballs on busy intersections with multiple lights. The biggest drawback with bandit signs is that cities have cracked down on their usage and now remove them on a regular basis. Find out what day your city or state sends out cleanup teams to take down signs and remove yours before they get trashed (or just let the cleanup teams take care of it). I've heard of sting operations in which enforcement officers pose as sellers just to determine who is the owner of a bandit sign. Instead of getting a juicy contract, you'll get a juicy fine.

Many start-up wholesalers rely on bandit signs for their acquisitions funnel because they're both cost-effective and efficient in getting your phone to ring. My team has never used bandit signs for one simple fact: I'm too lazy for that and I don't expect my staff to do it. However, some of the most successful wholesalers consistently use bandit signs to generate new leads. Spencer Bishop of Avila Palms properties often uses bandit signs in his business. Here are a few of his tips:

- Bandit signs work primarily in smaller markets. For Spencer, larger cities, like Tampa and Orlando, aren't as profitable because code enforcement, city officials, homeowners, and even competitors would routinely pick up and discard signs before they could be monetized.
- Bandit signs do, however, work in smaller, more rural areas with the following KPIs:
  - Average cost per sign = $4.31
  - Average cost per deal = $2,866.66

TV and Radio Ads

TV and radio ads have been a tried-and-true source of lead generation for decades, but they can be costly. One major benefit is this medium's scale and opportunity to create brand visibility. The average campaign costs $10,000 a month, with a term minimum and an average cost per contract of around $6,700. These costs are similar to the costs of direct mail. It's difficult to gauge the value of brand recognition gained through TV and radio ads because the feedback loop is so much broader, but I can tell you that J.G. Wentworth is who you call when "it's your money and you want it now."

Doug Hopkins, a local celebrity wholesaler in Phoenix, Arizona, shared his costs:

- Average cost per contract = $6,700.
- Average cost per lead = $500.
- Close at 10 percent on average = $30,000 leads to 4.5 deals.
  - Aim for 2.0 return on ad spend to guide spending goals.

Door Knocking/Driving for Dollars

This is an old-school technique for generating leads. Whether it was encyclopedias, knives, or vacuum cleaners, this method goes way back. However, this technique requires you to be proactive because your results are directly tied to how many homes you reach. It requires little to no cash investment to implement this strategy because the majority of the investment comes in the form of your time. There are still some costs involved with obtaining lists, buying supportive shoes, paying for gas and car upkeep, and so on, but the costs associated with this strategy are still much less than other forms of transactional/paid marketing. The KPIs for door knocking/driving for dollars range on the type of lead list. The most effective door-knocking campaigns are properties in pre-foreclosure. The cost of these lists is minimal and oftentimes can be obtained for free from your local title company. Again, that means that outside of the costs just mentioned, door knocking offers the lowest cost per contract of any the transactional approaches discussed.

As you now know, transactional approaches range in cost from low to quite hefty, but they do work. However, not everyone is cut out for this type of "hunter" business model. People with great communication skills, organization, discipline, and negotiation will excel in this form of marketing because it allows you to get in close with a seller and negotiate the best possible outcome for them and your business.

The main thing to note is that the transactional strategy rarely leads to multiple deals with the same seller, so you'll need to continue to spend time and money on this method to grow your business.

RELATIONAL STRATEGY

This strategy revolves around the long-term mutual benefit for both parties, in which individuals work toward a mutually beneficial solution and are incentivized to strengthen their relationship by minimizing their self-interest.

In wholesale acquisitions, the two most popular working relationships are with:

- Real estate agents.
- Other wholesalers.

Real Estate Agents

A real estate agent is a person who represents sellers or buyers of real estate or real property. In 1908, the National Association of Real Estate Exchanges was founded to bring agents together to facilitate the buying and selling of homes. The idea of advocating for home buying and selling is long established, so real estate investors like wholesalers seek to create mutually beneficial relationships, and we often have real estate agents at the top of our lists.

When someone is thinking about selling their house, the first person they often contact is a real estate agent. All agency relationships are fiduciary relationships. According to *Black's Law Dictionary*, a fiduciary duty is defined as "a duty of utmost good faith, trust, confidence, and candor owed by a fiduciary to the beneficiary; a duty to act with the highest degree of honesty and loyalty toward another person and in the best interests of the other person." Since real estate agents are charged with the duty of finding the best solution in the interest of their clients, working with a wholesaler may be the most prudent solution for them.

Earlier in this chapter I mentioned the real estate agent who referred a foreclosure situation to me. When the agent could no longer help the homeowner with the foreclosure, they were acting in the best interest of that homeowner because they knew a traditional sale would never solve that situation given the timing. Real estate agents will weigh all the factors of their client's situation and typically present them with multiple options to choose between. When a real estate agent and a wholesaler work together, the relationship has one of two forms. One is that the agent represents the seller, from whom you want to get the right to the property, in which case they are trying to get the best price and terms for their seller. Or they represent the buyer, to whom you want to sell that right, so their duty will be in the interest of the buyer.

A quick note here about the terms "real estate agent" and "Realtor." These terms are often used interchangeably, but they are different. The main difference is that Realtors (always spelled with a capital R) are members of the National Association of Realtors.® Real estate agents can and do become Realtors. Realtors must follow the codes of ethics set by the NAR; real estate agents do not.

The key benefit to working with a real estate agent or Realtor is that their primary business is working with property owners. An active real estate agent will prospect up to fifty property owners in any given workday, and the likelihood of one or more of those prospects needing the services of a wholesaler is high. Now take that same line of thinking and apply it to a real estate investor. A real estate investor who focuses on working with active real estate agents could network with fifty agents a day. The effective reach of an investor who networks with fifty agents a day who network with fifty property owners a day equals 2,500 potential property owners per day. That number is staggering!

Real estate agents are one of my main sources of leads. And the best part is that working with real estate agents is free.

Let me give you a personal example. One key relationship I have is with Monique Walker, a real estate agent in Phoenix. Monique and I do dozens of deals a year to the point where I could have a million-dollar-a-year business just working with her. Imagine having this type of business while working with one person. Now, you can build a network with dozens of real estate agents like Monique, giving you the foundation for an eight-figure real estate operation.

Building these relationships centers on a process I call agent outreach. This strategy involves cold-calling and texting real estate agents to find out if they have any leads on original condition or dated properties that have been sitting on the market or are coming to market soon that could use a cash offer. What's most exciting about agent outreach is that it's a business-to-business lead-generation process. Real estate agents spend a tremendous amount of money advertising themselves to get their name and phone number out there. It's thus rare to have a real estate agent not want to talk to you when you're contacting them about business. The same certainly cannot be said when cold-calling homeowners. I could fill another book with all of the swear words wholesalers have been called over the phone when cold-calling, making this an unenjoyable process. Yes, I did describe this earlier as a method of contact but know that it isn't the easiest one.

Here is KeyGlee's Agent Outreach funnel:

1. **Outreach Text 1:** Outreach with short intro on what you're seeking.

   Examples:

   "Hi Dan, my name's Jamil. Could you help me with a purchase?"

   "Hey Janice, my name is Jamil and I'm looking for fixer-upper opportunities in the greater Phoenix Metro area. Do you happen to have or know of any?"

   "Hi Carl! Are you still in real estate and taking new clients? I'm looking to make a purchase. Jamil."

   "Hey Christine! This is Jamil, and I am looking for my next off-market deal. Would love to be a buyer for you. Do you have anything available coming up?"

2. **Outreach Text 2:** Follow-up sent to anyone who didn't respond, usually the following day.

   "Hey! Just following up on my text from yesterday. Are you still in real estate?"

   "Hey Randy, I'm looking for my next fixer-upper. Can you help me with that?"

3. Call anyone who didn't respond to either outreach text.

Best practices for agent outreach:
- Be confident.
- Use "I," not "we." You are the one sending the messages and making the calls.
- Don't answer questions they didn't ask.
- Avoid the urge to overexplain; embrace the silence.
- Allow the conversation to flow naturally.
- Ask them to save your number, then text you info.

Agent follow-up strategies:
- Bi-monthly check-in text:
  - We send these in bulk to follow up with more agents.
  - Use simple text to stay top of mind.
  - Rewrite your messages daily to avoid getting flagged as spam.

Negotiating the deal:
- Try not to give your price first.
- Give them an anchor price, then negotiate up to your top dollar (if need be).
- You're negotiating with the agent. Ask them to run it by their client, the seller.
- Use favorable terms instead of coming up in price:
  - "What if I were to waive the buyer's side commission?"
  - "What will it take to get the deal done today?"

Agent outreach KPIs:
- Fifty conversations per eight-hour workday.
- Call duration not to exceed six minutes.
- Average number of follow-ups per contract is eight to thirteen.
- Average number of days from first contact to contract is ninety days.
- Average cost per contract is $0.

Other Wholesalers

Wholesaling's popularity as an entry point for real estate investing business has exploded. People just getting started are looking for business opportunities that allow them the freedom to make uncapped income and to participate in real estate transactions, all without needing access to a lot of funds, good credit, or a real estate license. Because of that, there are a lot of classes on the internet teaching people how to participate in wholesale. Most teachers are experienced wholesalers showing people the path to success. I think all of that education is amazing.

The problem, however, is that others are using this popularity to grab quick cash from would-be entrepreneurs who have no experience in the business. Because of this, there is a tremendous amount of misinformation on YouTube, TikTok, Instagram, and Facebook. These "influencers" only want to sell courses and push their affiliates. How are you to know the difference between worthwhile and worthless training?

As you have figured out, I have nothing against making money. And I also have a wholesale real estate community that costs money to join. I believe that investing in yourself is important. I think joining a community of like-minded individuals who are going along the same journey as you is the fastest path to success. I teach newbies for free because I believe that everyone who has the desire to do this business should have all the tools and resources available to them without charge. The costs should be after you enter the business with your eyes open. The silver lining is that the new people coming into this industry are already networked with the other students who took the training at the same time. The right classes also provide forums to collaborate with experienced wholesalers.

Here's an example. A wannabe wholesaler watches a video on YouTube and learns how to pull a list for cold calling, how to vet for the types of buyers or sellers they're looking for, and how to start making phone calls to those who match the criteria. That's all good. What's not good is that they aren't taught how to properly assess the current or potential value of any property. And they don't know anyone who can do this. Or the new wholesaler finds a qualified property to put under contract, but they weren't taught how to find a cash buyer. Without a cash buyer, the deal will most certainly fall through. This is why networking is as important as the training. New wholesalers must know how to collaborate and work with others in the industry to get the deal done.

When wholesalers begin to scale their business, it's human nature that they focus on the skills that they are most proficient at. Rarely do you find wholesalers who are talented at acquisitions and underwriting (the money part) and dispositions (finding the buyers). That means there's tremendous opportunities for collaboration when wholesalers and others bring skills to the table that their counterparts don't have.

KeyGlee was founded because my other three founders and I noticed a vacuum in the wholesale space in Phoenix. In 2016, a lot of acquisition wholesalers were canceling their contracts with homeowners because they couldn't find buyers for their deals. We saw this as a golden opportunity to become a one-stop-shop solution for wholesalers nationwide. There was no effective way to build connections in the wholesale space. We wanted acquisition wholesalers to focus on their specific skill set without having to risk cancellations of their contracts because they couldn't find buyers. Today, KeyGlee is known for being the go-to wholesaler disposition franchise for wholesalers across the United States.

This idea of collaboration over competition has allowed our company and many other companies to increase their connectivity, networking, and bottom lines by increasing the volume of transactions and assignment fees. With relationships with other wholesalers, it's possible to close dozens of deals every single month. In our case, KeyGlee makes nearly $20,000 on every transaction that we close. As I noted about my relationship with Monique Walker earlier in this chapter, that one relationship brings in millions of dollars for both of us. Now, imagine having dozens of relationships with real estate agents and other wholesalers. That's the power of networking. And this is why getting training online without the chance to network with other students is only half the education.

As someone new to wholesale, you need to build relationships to create your funnel and to bring in deals.
- Get to know the real estate agents in your area.
- Seek out wholesaler experts.
- Wholesalers know of properties not typically on the MLS.
- Once you build trust, they will send you deals.

Outreach KPIs to aim for:
- Fifty conversations per eight-hour workday.
- Call duration should not exceed six minutes.
- Average number of follow-ups per 1 contract = 3.
- Average number of days from first contact to contract = 7 days.
- Average cost per contract = $0.

Here is KeyGlee's wholesaler outreach funnel:

- We provide the resources like earnest money deposit (EMD), proof of funds, and a credible track record.
  - We have constant communication at least once a week.
  - We run the numbers to confirm the math; not every deal is a deal, but we never say no without doing the homework.
- We follow up with wholesalers who haven't responded from the previous day or that morning (see Outreach Text 1 examples earlier in this chapter).
- We review our current pipeline to check if deals are still available.
- We check low-hanging fruit.
  - We review wholesale lists.
  - We check out Facebook investor groups.
- We follow up with wholesalers on specific deals.
  - Examples:
    "I have one coming up in Chandler next week."
    "Check back next week."
- Busy wholesalers and agents need more frequent follow-up calls and texts.

How to Find Acquisition Wholesalers

Acquisition wholesalers can be found in many ways. I continue to find new ways to meet wholesalers, even after years in the business. The following outlines some of the platforms and strategies I've found useful for networking opportunities.

FACEBOOK GROUPS

Facebook groups offer the most plentiful resources for wholesalers, hands down. Almost every community group, influencer, and local networking event has an accompanying group on Facebook to share ideas and experiences and to collaborate. For example, Max Maxwell has Wholesaling Houses Elite, with over 150,000 members. And every member is a potential deal connection. My AstroFlipping community has about 16,000 members, all of whom are ready to collaborate with other wholesalers on deals.

There are also regional Facebook groups that are specific to local markets. These can be tremendous resources. However, be careful about how you approach and message people in these groups. Facebook's security protocols are strict, and spamming members in different communities is frowned upon. Ensure the number of messages you send does not exceed the current parameters of the site's messaging limits. I also highly recommend that you use a Facebook profile that has been long established. People often believe that they need to create a separate profile for their business to keep their business and personal lives apart. The problem with this is business profiles often contain no information, with limited to no posting history, and thus a more inactive profile. This creates a lack of credibility. When people receive messages from a skeleton Facebook profile, they may suspect it's a bot rather than a real person. What usually holds people back from integrating their business and personal profiles is fear of judgment from family and friends. Likewise, they may be worried about how potential real estate investors they want to work with might interpret elements from their personal life. In this case, I recommend browsing through your profile from an objective point of view and deleting anything you wouldn't want a future business partner to see.

Don't be afraid to announce in your personal profile that you're a real estate investor. If you do not believe in your ability to succeed, you will always find ways to sabotage your success. Take a step back to Chapter 4 when I talk about mindset and how you view business and value. Embrace your decision to become a wholesaler and your new identity as a real estate investor. Post openly about your business, your wins, and your losses. Those who judge, let them judge. If you lose their friendship, they were never really your friends in the first place. The people who support you will inquire about your day-to-day wins and losses. Plus, you never know when a family member or friend might have a troubled property they need help with. Why not be their rescuer?

INSTAGRAM AND TIKTOK

It would be impossible for me to count the millions of dollars my company has made through my own Instagram profile. As I share my journey as a wholesaler, I have been DM'd thousands of times by people with opportunities, people who want to network, and people who want to connect on deals. Before I had a name in this wholesale world, I was unknown. I used my Instagram account as a tool to connect with people and to share this journey with its wins and losses. In the process, it helped me build a huge community of wholesalers.

Pay attention to influencers in your preferred market, and see who's liking their posts and who's making comments. Then connect with those people. It's worth your time to engage with people who inspire you. "Like" their posts, send DMs, make comments, etc. Check trending hashtags or topics in the search bar, and pay attention to what hashtags the people you're following use. (For those not on social media, you'll need to start using it and learning its lexicon.) Going down a rabbit hole on Instagram and TikTok to connect with like-minded business owners can be quite lucrative and has the potential to help you build a future network worth its weight in gold.

NETWORKING EVENTS, IN-PERSON AND VIRTUAL

There are many in-person events held by educators, influencers, course creators, and software creators. These are often designed to sell you coaching or subscription services. That doesn't matter. Attend anyway. Expect to be sold to at these types of events, but your true goal is to network with other attendees. That's the real value of these events. Some of the larger events (such as BPCON, the annual BiggerPockets conference) can have upward of 3,000 attendees; connecting with just 2 percent of that audience could means millions of dollars in business for you. Attend these events with the intention to meet people, not to spend your money on training, software, or anything else. Set your expectations to meet like-minded wholesalers. I often recommend that wholesale companies purchase both in-person and virtual tickets to events for their staff, as the attendance numbers can be greater in the virtual sessions. Virtual sessions have the incredibly powerful addition of connecting with people through the comment section, where they can talk about themselves and even leave their business URLs, email addresses, and social media handles.

Here's a personal example of how this works. One of my community members was unable to attend the 2022 10X event in Hollywood, Florida, in person, so he bought a virtual ticket. That investor networked with thousands of real estate investors in the chat and connected with another attendee to collaborate on development for a self-storage facility. These two went on to sell that contract for a $500,000 profit. The cost of those virtual tickets? $90 each. Do the math—the return on investment can be tremendously high.

LIVE STREAMS AND PODCASTS

Every week, I cohost a live-stream podcast called *Wholesale Hotline* with Pace Morby and Brent Daniels. We routinely have over 1,000 viewers join us live every Monday. That has resulted in millions of dollars of deals getting started among attendees who use the live chat. Joining in on live streams and podcasts—such as *Real Estate Disruptors; Wholesaling Inc.; Get Creative with Pace Morby;* and many others—is free. There are no memberships and no tickets to buy. The ROI for your time and effort is infinite.

LOCAL REAL ESTATE INVESTOR ASSOCIATION

Almost every major city has a real estate investor association, or REIA. These typically operate as nonprofit organizations, although they do collect dues to cover overhead costs and expenses, such as food and possibly guest speakers. I've made tremendous relationships attending the REIA in Phoenix, whether through networking, finding vendors, or simply looking for deals. Wholesalers can connect with cash buyers, real estate agents, and other wholesalers to build their business network. I strongly suggest that you, as a new wholesaler, seek out the local REIA in your region, and then participate by volunteering and making yourself a known member. This will escalate the connections you make. REIAs are also a great way to make connections to lenders, title companies, contractors, and buyers, so be prepared to meet as many people and take as many numbers as possible. Although I find business cards archaic, this is an exception: Having one here gives you the opportunity to leave your contact information with individuals. Make sure that your social media profiles are set up prior to attending, so you don't miss any connections with those who don't save or collect business cards.

For instance, I met a buyer at a REIA who I've been working with now for over eight years. Jack and I have done dozens of transactions and made hundreds of thousands of dollars together. We've become close friends, but we could not be more different from each other. Jack is in his late 70s, runs marathons, and spends his winters in Hawaii. I do none of those things. We come from quite different demographics. In fact, without being in our REIA, we never would have met because our lives run in opposite directions. If we hadn't met, we never would have become friends and working colleagues. The point in this example is to seek relationships with people who are not like you, who look different than you, and who are in different age groups than you. Judge no one. You just don't know where that next deal is coming from.

Have many conversations, ask many questions, and engage in conversations with value. Add the value of your unique perspective to any conversation you're having.

INDUSTRY-SPECIFIC SOCIAL MEDIA PLATFORMS

Forums within platforms like BiggerPockets are incredible resources to find like-minded investors who may have wholesale opportunities or who could be potential property buyers. Connecting with and corresponding with members on these forums can fast-track the number of relationships you make with high-level people. Some of the greatest real estate relationships I've made have come from my association with BiggerPockets. Additionally, these platforms often host yearly conventions that attract thousands of attendees. Engage with these platforms and contribute by adding value at every opportunity. The more active you are, the more people know you, the bigger your network gets, and the more business you will do. No real estate deal has ever happened with just one person. Use the power of networking and collaboration to build your presence and overall business.

POP-UPS AND MEETUPS

Pop-ups and meetups happen regularly within the wholesaling community. These events are less structured and organized but are still fruitful avenues to connect with other investors in your local area. Meetups are usually spearheaded by social media influencers, so pay attention to who are the movers and shakers in your local area and follow their social media feeds. Set the intention to meet at least ten to twenty people. Speaking as an influencer who creates these types of events, I can honestly tell you that I would much rather see you networking with multiple attendees and finding ways to extend your business than have you standing in line waiting to take a picture with me. Your goal should be to connect with as many people as possible to add to your network.

There are only two things that you need to do to make a networking event worth it for yourself: Ask questions and then listen. That's it, and it seems so simple. Yet a lot of the attendees either just want to meet the host, talk to the most newsworthy guest speaker, find where the cool kids are in the room, or aren't prepared to speak to anyone at all. Interacting with others opens so many doors of opportunity, so if you're like the last type mentioned, bury your shyness for an hour or two. The bottom line is focusing on how you can deliver value to someone. Remember, when we deliver value, we receive value in return. For every event, you'll always find someone to meet and potentially network with, including:

- Other wholesalers.
- Real estate agents.
- Fix-and-flippers
- Lenders.
- Vendors.
- Title companies.
- Other investors.

Acquisition Wholesaling

Acquisition wholesalers spend a lot of time talking and meeting with sellers, buyers, and other investors and I'll get into disposition wholesaling in a later chapter, but for now, here are some pros and cons to becoming an acquisition wholesaler:

ACQUISITION PROS

- You control the deal.
- You control the title.
  - This includes benefits, perks, lists, legal, discounts, and relationships.
- You have control over paperwork.
- The spreads are larger.
- Dispo wholesalers will court you.

ACQUISITION CONS

- Marketing expenses are high.
- You must depend on buyer to perform.
- You must do work before money is on the table.
  - This can be risky for the effort involved.
- The business is feast or famine.
  - You're always chasing the next seller.

ACQUISITIONS IN THE WILD

Earlier in this chapter you learned about transactional and relational strategies, and that the latter is the one that can result in a lifetime of collaborations. In June 2022, I connected Andy, a KeyGlee acquisitions specialist, with Albaro, a longtime friend. During the week, Albaro manages a successful podiatrist office in his home country of Canada, and on the weekends he's good at finding real estate deals. Andy tells the story:

> What Albaro is great at is spotting a good deal. He's also learned how to have good conversations with real estate agents. I backed Albaro with cash funds, so he could now make offers feeling confident he/we could perform. He went out and did what he was trained to do—agent outreach.
>
> Albaro came to me and said, "Hey, I've been following up with this really awesome agent with a great project house on

the MLS that was listed for $650,000 for months and has now been reduced to $620,000. It's a fixer-upper so retail buyers just keep passing on it, saying it needs too much work, but it's priced really well. If we fixed up the home, it could sell for $900,000." Albaro saw the potential. After running the numbers for the property, we felt comfortable to back his offer for $620,000. Albaro contracted the property and sold the contract to KeyGlee for $635,000. KeyGlee was able to find a fix-and-flip buyer at $650,000. The fix-and-flipper who bought this property didn't have the time to search the MLS all day for deals, as he is always busy on job sites. Albaro helped the seller finally sell their home that sat stale for months, and he made $15,000 for his efforts. KeyGlee got a project in the hands of a longtime client and also made $15K.

To this day, Coleman—the agent Albaro works with—still sends Albaro deals and Albaro still sells us deals as well.

This is a prime example of a relational approach to lead generation. Here, a real estate agent worked with a wholesaler to solve a seller's needs when traditional tools weren't working. Retail buyers in the area weren't interested in a fixer-upper. Fix-and-flip specialists were busy on other projects. Albaro "squaded up" with KeyGlee through Andy to ensure access to the funds needed to deliver the solution. It also showcases something I mentioned previously: collaboration, not competition. It would have been easy for Andy to just work directly with the agent Coleman and cut out Albaro. However, Andy wouldn't have even known of the deal without Albaro's efforts, so everyone earned their place at the table. The honesty earned relationship equity with Albaro to do future deals with us. Also note that if Coleman had avoided working with a wholesaler, the house wouldn't have found its ideal buyer. The MLS had listed the property for months, with no one showing interest. The seller may not have received $620,000 because further reductions would have been the only method to attract attention.

As Andy explains, he and Albaro have built a lasting and profitable relationship. They've worked on many other deals together since, and Coleman continues to bring new opportunities after learning the value of working with ethical wholesalers. This is just one example of how a long-lasting relational approach can work for acquisition wholesalers.

Closing a Seller and Completing a Contract

Acquisition wholesalers need to use empathy and understanding when asking the four main questions that must be asked of every potential seller:

- What is the condition of your property?
- What is your timeline?
- What is your motivation?
- What is your expectation of price?

WHAT IS THE CONDITION OF YOUR PROPERTY?

Remember that as wholesalers, you're looking for houses that have an opportunity for potential. You'll need to find out if the owner has made any recent repairs or renovations that remove that potential. Ask yourself: Is there an opportunity to add value to this property?

WHAT IS YOUR TIMELINE?

Sellers will often trade value for speed, so you'll want to understand their timeline. Are they facing impending bills, foreclosure, relocation, or other distressed situations? These types of sellers want their home sold as quickly as possible, so their timeline is much shorter than an average deal.

WHAT IS YOUR MOTIVATION?

Understanding why a seller wants to sell is extremely important to your conversation. Every seller wants to solve their problem; if they didn't, they wouldn't be talking to you in the first place. Our job is to help solve that problem, including finding a better price for their property.

WHAT IS YOUR EXPECTATION OF PRICE?

Many sellers go online to gain some insight as to how much their property might be worth. The challenge with using Zillow and other property tools as a basis is they can't account for needed repairs, renovations, or changes. Then they list the property at $125,000 when it's actually worth only $95,000. This is not the time to become argumentative and tell the seller why their numbers aren't realistic. What they tell you opens an opportunity for you to understand where they're starting from and how they got there. Acknowledge their resourcefulness, and then explain why the numbers aren't right for their situation. Sometimes people simply aren't realistic. If a seller wants to price their home far and above the realistic price, that's a good indicator that maybe they lack the right motivation to sell. Or maybe they are the perfect candidates for a gentle wake-up call to the opportunity for creative finance solutions out of their problem.

Creative Finance

Before I close out this chapter, I want to tell you about another option when it comes to deal structure. Occasionally, you'll find a seller who is stuck on pricing, or has too nice of a home, or has no potential equity on the table. If the seller is unwilling to negotiate on price, it may be an opportunity to buy the deal on terms. Pace Morby is known as the Creative Finance Guy due to his vast knowledge of creative real estate strategies. Pace has written on creative finance, and I highly recommend his book, *Wealth without Cash* (also published by BiggerPockets) because it teaches how to supercharge your real estate investing with subject-to financing, seller financing, and other creative deals. Like wholesaling, creative financing is a way to buy real estate without needing cash, credit, or credentials. I'll give you a surface-level introduction to the world of creative finance, but you should definitely read Pace's book for the whole story.

I will cover two of the most common methods of creative financing:

- Seller financing
- Subject-to financing

SELLER FINANCING

In seller financing, the seller of the home or property provides the loan to the buyer. Essentially, the seller becomes the bank and the buyer makes payments directly to the seller, usually on a monthly basis. Payment schedule, payment amount, and length of time are all decided upon by the seller and buyer, and the terms are usually contracted to provide documentation of the deal.

SUBJECT-TO FINANCING

In subject-to financing, a buyer takes title to a property subject to an existing loan that remains in the name of the seller. For example, if a seller has an existing FHA, VA, or conventional loan with a bank, the buyer takes over those payments and makes them directly in place of the seller. Subject-to financing can greatly relieve financial stress on a seller who is looking to sell their home but is unable to negotiate on price.

Here's an example of how creative financing works. Pace had a truck sitting in his driveway that his wife, Laura, wanted him to sell. He checked the Kelley Blue Book, which listed his truck as worth $5,000. Pace was emotionally attached to the vehicle and refused to let it go for that little. He originally posted the truck for sale on Craigslist for $10,000, but he quickly discovered that people weren't willing to pay that price. His truck sat on different marketplace sites being completely ignored for months. Eventually, Laura reminded Pace that he is the Creative Finance Guy and that maybe he needed to think outside the box. That sparked an idea to sell his truck using seller financing. Pace changed his ad to read "will take payments," and immediately his phone began to buzz with interest. He ended up selling the truck that same day. Pace sold the truck to a painter who planned to use the vehicle for work, and Pace accepted monthly payments. Pace sold the truck for a total of $12,500, far more than he originally asked for, simply by taking payments.

Pace frequently uses subject-to financing to help homeowners in distressed situations. One couple had just bought a home on a large acre of land and were on the verge of retirement. Sadly, shortly afterward, they both had COVID-19 and the husband died from health complications. Now, this situation was bad enough, but to make matters worse the husband was the sole income provider, which meant that his death triggered a host of financial problems that the wife wasn't expecting. In the midst of this horrible tragedy, she fell behind on her monthly payments and was at risk of losing her home. Pace learned about the situation and used subject-to financing to buy the property over market value, which helped the homeowner relocate to her son's home and receive the cash she needed with no other income to rely on. Pace took over the $1,800 monthly mortgage payments (having assumed her loan) and then rented out the home for $2,800 per month. He overpaid for the property, which helped the seller out of her horrible predicament and he made money from the deal. It was a win-win for everyone.

In both of these scenarios, creative financing worked for the seller in distress (the wife) and the seller unwilling to negotiate on price (Pace). In the latter case, Pace secured three times the standard market value for his truck. In the former, the house and property sold for over market value. This was not a wholesale acquisition—Pace wasn't looking for the potential. He was seeing how creative financing could prevent a foreclosure and leave a widow with opportunity while creating a rental opportunity for himself.

When to Use Creative Financing

Wholesale situations with distressed sellers usually call for creative financing, but there are a few other cases where it might also be useful. Let's say an investor wants to purchase a home that has an ARV of $200,000, but the seller owes their lender $200,000. In this example, the seller would owe equal to, if not more than, the house's maximum potential value. The saving grace is that the seller's loan is a low 2.75 percent rate, which means the seller's monthly mortgage payment is relatively low. The seller has no money to make repairs or room to negotiate other options, which would scare away most investors. Most real estate agents would also walk away because there would be no commission. However, a buy-and-hold investor might determine the average monthly rent, and as long as their loan payment is less, the property could cash-flow. This deal would require no or low money down, yet create a monthly cash-flow from nothing. But you need to have the right elements such as a low interest rate and entry fee as well as an opportunity to cashflow from monthly rent to make this work.

If a deal doesn't make sense, then by all means walk away. But if a deal can generate a healthy cash flow, then by all means go for it. Overpaying on a deal that won't make you money is bad business. You can have empathy for people in rough situations, and creative financing can offer options when the numbers don't make sense at first glance. However, as discussed in Chapter 4, if you feel inclined to adjust the value of what you should earn depending on who the deal is with (such as family or friends), then you need to revisit your relationship with the financial aspect of your business and what your time and skills are truly worth.

In the above example, a wholesaler can assign or sell a deal structured with creative finance to generate a large single payday … or keep the property as a rental.

WHOLESALE SUCCESS STORY
The Agent Outreach Method with Michelle Garabito

Can you imagine closing multiple deals while traveling the world? How about getting a notification from your bank that $20,000 just hit your account while you're on a flight to your dream destination? I don't have to imagine, because that's exactly what happens to me multiple times a month, every single month.

My name is Michelle Garabito. I'm 31 years old, and here is my story on how with zero experience in real estate, I escaped a toxic work environment and created over half a million dollars in profit through assignment fees with my boyfriend and business partner, Paul Nelson, over the last two years. Our deals happen through two markets (Colorado and Tennessee). We run our businesses virtually and create these results using the agent outreach method.

When I first learned about wholesaling, the focus was on the old-school way of getting distressed properties under contract through door knocking, driving for dollars, bandit signs, mailers, and cold-calling. While I'm sure those methods work for many people, I knew there had to be a better, smarter, and more efficient way to get leads. This was important to Paul and me because we travel full-time—you won't see us door knocking when we're living in Asia! We knew we had to figure out better ways to get homes under contract so we can get consistent deal flow.

Finally, we found a way in Jamil Damji's agent outreach method. When we first started this process, we took nine steps to gain massive momentum:

1. Talk to five to ten agents a day.
2. Explain to them exactly what type of homes we were looking for.
3. Tell the agents what their workflow should be (sending us two to five deals a day).
4. Submit offers on at least three of them, or the best ones.
5. Communicate with the agent on how the contracting process is going.
6. Follow up every day and every week.
7. Get two to three deals under contract weekly.
8. Close four deals a month.
9. Rinse and Repeat.

I stayed consistent with this workflow until I had five excellent agents who I built great relationships with sending me great deals they can represent me on if I offer. The relationship with these agents is so key because they are now focusing on sending me great deals and working with me to get the right price for every deal. They are also giving me priority in their business. With my network of buyers and my ability to value properties, I realized that to continue to grow agent relationships, I have to make sure I assign or close on the deals myself and stay consistent to create win-win opportunities. This is very important.

The best deal I ever did utilizing our agent relationships was in Colorado Springs, Colorado. For this specific deal, our top agent followed her daily workflow with me and sent me an amazing deal on a beautiful summer day. My acquisitions manager ran the numbers to make sure it was at a good price for us to move it and make a decent assignment fee. Our agent spoke to the listing agent and built a good relationship with her to ensure she prioritized our offer. Since we'd closed over a dozen deals with this agent already, the confidence she exudes when representing us is a huge plus to other agents—she identifies my company and me as being credible, able to close, and trustworthy with transactions. This deal had also been sitting on the market for more than a month, so the listing agent and her seller were desperate to get it off their hands. Within three days, we got the property under contract at $815,000. This was a high-end deal: a four-bed, four-bath, 4,928 sq. ft. property in Colorado Springs.

Our agent took care of the negotiation with the listing agent and the seller; she even handled the paperwork. We just had to sign and get ready to perform on the contract. We intented to wholesale the contract because we were on our way to Hawaii for a month and we weren't going to take on any large projects.

I partnered up with Erik Piñuelas, whose buyers list had a good amount of buyers that can handle such a big rehab project. Most of my buyers were feeling conservative and didn't have the bandwidth to take on something of this proportion. We assigned the deal to Erik's buyer for $862,500, and seven days later (and the day before Erik's wedding), the deal closed and funded. Our assignment fee was $47,500, so Erik and I each took home $23,750. Partnerships and relationships in all forms got this deal closed and funded.

Fun fact: Today, that deal is on the market for $1.3 million. Win, win, win!

Imagine doing deals like this multiple times a month. It truly changed our life. Because of agent relationships like this, our wholesale business profits $50,000 a month. We get to live the life of our dreams. From starting our journey living in Mexico to then making more money and expanding our travels to the Maldives, Italy, Greece, Turkey, Thailand, Japan, and more, we couldn't have done it if it weren't for the agent outreach method and the guidance of Jamil Damji.

Please follow our journey on Instagram @michellegarabito @cr3ateabundance.

A QUICK RECAP

- The two main strategies to wholesale acquisition are transactional and relational.
- Transactional revolves around cost and benefits (ads, etc.).
- Relational revolves around long-term mutual benefits for both parties.
- Look for networking possibilities on social media platforms and by listening to podcasts and attending REIA and other meetup groups.
- Follow up quickly and consistently via text, email, and phone calls.
- Creative financing is a strategy to get deals done.

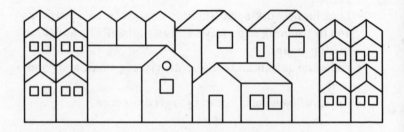

CHAPTER 6
Understanding Value

Throughout the book, I've talked about finding the potential value in properties most people wouldn't give a second glance. Sellers always believe their property or homes have "top of the market" value, so part of our job as wholesalers is to recognize and honor that emotional attachment while explaining a realistic view of the "as-is" value. Home, to use the saying, is where our heart is. It's where we have family gatherings like BBQs; celebrate birthdays, anniversaries, and holidays; and have good times with friends. Maybe we got married in the backyard, maybe our children were raised there. For some people, our homes are generational, having been passed down from a grandfather or great-grandfather who built the home. And while there may have been renovations over the years, it's still the same place where our grandparents read to us or where we learned how to bake and cook. Homes are often sentimental assets, and selling that particular asset can be hard. This can be especially true for those going through challenges and are forced into the process.

The family home I grew up in had a sunken living room where I used to play. The sentimental value of that space is what made the house special to me. In reality, a property investor might see this space as a huge cost because buyers today don't want sunken living rooms, so it would need to be leveled with the rest of the floor. What was a place of happiness for me decades ago is now a headache to be fixed by $5,000 in concrete work.

One fundamental concept every wholesaler must learn is how to determine if a wholesale deal is worth it. To do that, we must determine both the current and potential values in that property using specific calculations that help find the right price for you, your buyer, and the seller. This chapter covers the important concept of how to compare your subject property with others in a neighborhood. I explain the process of comping, where it comes from, why we do it, and, more importantly, how to do it correctly and accurately.

What Is Comping?

Comping is the art of comparing aspects of the subject house to similar homes in a neighborhood by using historical sales data to help determine value; in other words, it compares similar characteristics of recently sold properties. This process of comparison continues until we have built a "case for value" based on sales evidence, usually on homes sold within ninety calendar days of each other. We then use this same process to build a case for after repair value based on improvements. This sounds like a simple task, but many real estate professionals get this part wrong. I've surveyed hundreds of Realtors on this subject and have met only a handful who learned the art of comping in licensing courses.

Comping is comparing apples-to-apples characteristics. If you're looking at a single-story three-bedroom, two-bathroom home that's 3,200 square feet and built in the 1950s, you cannot compare it to a two-story four-bedroom, three-bathroom home with 4,200 square feet built in the 2000s.

And yet I have seen situations where this has happened.

I absolutely believe that knowing how to comp and being able to do it effectively and efficiently is a fundamental of our business. To comp accurately, you must derive the value of the properties that interest you. Honestly, the biggest dream killer for 99.9 percent of new wholesalers is their first deal getting canceled. This often happens because either they don't understand what a property is realistically worth or what it will realistically cost to make it match a renovated comparable. Incorrect comping or costing leads to canceled contracts. And canceled contracts perpetuate the stigma that wholesalers aren't serious buyers.

The foundation of my professional success derives from my obsession with mastering the art of comping. Appraisers are trained and licensed to estimate the value of a property, and one of the best ways to develop your comping ability is understanding how appraisers determine value through appraisal rules.

What Are Appraisal Rules?

Very simply, they're the rules that appraisers use when assigning a value to a property or property's characteristics. Appraisers are hired by lenders to evaluate and determine property value. It's important for a wholesaler to follow these rules because the eventual buyer of your contract will be subjected to this process when selling their renovated project or refinancing their loan.

There are multiple criteria that appraisers use when it comes to appraising property. The following information is based on my talking with hundreds of appraisers.

APPRAISAL RULES

NEW FOR 2023:

USE COMPS NO OLDER THAN 90 DAYS
OLDER COMPS: ADJUST ARV DOWN 10%-20%
TO ACCOMMODATE MARKET CORRECTION

SAME SUBDIVISION
+/- 250 SQUARE FEET
SAME PROPERTY TYPE (RANCH, 2-STORY, HISTORIC)
DO NOT CROSS ANY MAJOR ROADS
DO NOT USE A COMP MORE THAN +/- 10 YEARS OF
YOUR PROPERTY'S BUILD DATE
BETTER TO LEAVE SUBIVISION THAN TIME TRAVEL

ADJUSTMENTS
ONLY COMPARE HOME WITHIN 2,500 SQFT OF LOT SIZE

- BEDROOM +/- 25K
- BATHROOM +/- 10K
- POOL +/- 10K
- GARAGE +/- 10K
- CARPORT +/- 5K

TRAFFIC & COMMERCIAL

UNDER 500K
- SIDING - 10K
- BACKING - 10K
- FRONTING - 10K-20K

OVER 500K
- SIDING - 10%
- BACKING - 15%
- FRONTING - 20%

BASEMENT/GUEST HOUSE
ONLY GIVE 50% OF $/SQFT VALUE

If you need a Proof of Funds email: FlipFundLLC@gmail.com to get yours

© ASTROFLIPPING 2023

Let's break each section down.

Subdivision

Subdivisions are larger parcels of land that are divided into smaller lots because those are easier to sell or otherwise develop, usually via a plat. You can think of a subdivision as a small community. Typically subdivisions are developed within a consistent build generation of five to ten years, so aspects of materials and building technology are fairly consistent throughout a subdivision. This consistency is the basis on which value can be accurately derived. Per the appraisal rules, when you are comparing properties, your most likely match will be within the same subdivision. It's even common to find "model match" comparables that share identical architectural specifications and features. For example, master planned neighborhood communities often offer only a handful of model variations. This is not my favorite type of neighborhood aesthetically, but it sure makes it easy to determine value. The highest accuracy for finding viable comparables will be within the same subdivision.

Having similar square footage is also incredibly important when comparing homes. Your properties—your subject and your comp—need to be within, at most, plus or minus 250 square feet in size. What that means is if your subject property is 3,250 square feet, you can use a comp property that is between 3,000 and 3,500 square feet. You cannot accurately compare it to a property that is 4,250 square feet.

Another variable to consider is that the properties that you're comparing are the same property type. You cannot compare a one-story ranch-style home with a two-story townhome, or a property within a historic district with one outside of the district. Your comp *must* be in the same property type as your subject property. An easy way to ensure you're comparing appropriate properties is to not cross any major roads when comparing houses. A neighborhood across a major road can be completely different.

When considering appraisal rules to determine value, understand that some of these rules will be broken for complex valuations. Also consider that the more rules that are broken, the less accurate the valuation will be. An appraiser will explore and compare properties that are closer together before they leave the subdivision. However, in a shifting market, age of the comp is more important than distance. Let's look at an example of three-bedroom homes. Let's say that your subject property has all the same features as two other homes, but your subject home was built in 2002, and a comp was built in 2001 and another comp was built in 1992. Which of these comps works with your subject property? Of course, it's the first comp because it's within five years of construction. Remember square footage differences? Well, you also can't comp a property that's not within a certain year range because of the differences in construction, build materials, technology, etc. You wouldn't compare a property built in 1982 with one built in 2022. Construction materials were different in the 1980s, and you could get away with using certain materials, such as those with lead or asbestos, that you absolutely can't use today. And the 2022 home might have conveniences not even in existence in 1982, such as smart technology.

This is something that I see all the time with new wholesalers. They start doing mental gymnastics trying to find a comp that fits within the narrative of the potential deal or present a deal in the most favorable light to a buyer. They break the rules by finding comps that are outside of the subdivision, or have too much or too little square footage, are different property types, and so on. They try to justify the ARVs. This leads to pricing being too high and having that contract canceled with the seller because they can't find a buyer for the property.

When comparing properties, we want comps that have been sold within the last ninety days. There are a number of ways to find these properties, which I cover in the next chapter. You can go up to one mile out to find a recent comp. The key is that when leaving a subdivision that you are still comparing similar subdivisions. And knowing about active comps in other subdivisions is helpful because they can tell you about the inventory in a particular area. Is it a seller's market or a buyer's market? You can still use the rule of within five years of construction but be aware of the current market, and know that you must work within that market.

Note that lenders only offer loans on comparables that have already been sold. If there are no closed comps in the area that closely match your property or there is insufficient data to determine the value of your property, something else has to be done.

This is where adjustments come into play. Adjustments are made using the closest available comp to determine the value of your subject property when you don't have an exact match.

Adjustments

Since your appraisal cannot be based on a closed comparable, what do appraisers do?

For comps that are smaller than your potential buy, appraisers take the highest sale in the area and add an extra $10,000 to $15,000 for any additional square footage. They offer this extra amount on the highest subject property sold in that area, with the intent to avoid a lender or cash buyer from overpaying on a property of undetermined value.

Adjustments must also be made with comps that are bigger.

Appraisers look at the subdivision, property type, square footage, and construction year, and they also look for any changes that may have been made to the property. Adjustments include adding rooms, adding a garage or carport, or adding a pool. As you might expect, adjustments to a property add value to it.

When appraisers look at comparables, they also account for changes that could affect the pricing to determine the ARV. Here are the statistics on an example property:

- Single story.
- Three bedrooms.
- Two bathrooms.
- House is 1,765 square feet.
- Has two-car garage and a pool.
- Lot size of 3,200 square feet.

Let's say there is a home three doors down on the opposite side of the street that just sold:

- Single story.
- Four bedrooms.
- Two bathrooms.
- House is 1,850 square feet.
- Carport for two cars and no pool.
- Lot size of 3,200 square feet.

You would think you'd have to rule out this property as a comp because of the fourth bedroom, right? Not necessarily. This is where things get tricky. As you'll come to discover, no two properties are ever going to match perfectly. That's why there are caveats. In this case, the caveat is the extra bedroom. But you can't just pretend your property doesn't have a fourth bedroom.

Again, adjustments are made based on that comp's final sale price. For instance, if the comp sold for $350,000, then the appraiser would subtract $10,000 from that sale to price your subject property. If the comp sold for $500,000, then the adjustment downward would be $25,000.

Always refer to the appraiser rules when making these types of adjustments.

Traffic and Commercial

It's not just the numbers of bedrooms and bathrooms that get added to adjustments. There's also the location of a property. Let's say that you found a deal with a distressed property that's in an area that's been redeveloped with schools and playgrounds. You want to adjust accordingly for the property being in that improved location.

An appraiser may take into account types of traffic or commercial influences, depending on the area. For example, the Airport Zoning Act was established to set the rules for the use of land within a certain distance of an airport. It was enacted because of the growth of aviation and the need to ensure the safety and efficiency of air travel. Plus, most people don't enjoy the sounds of airplanes constantly flying at all hours, so there aren't a lot of neighborhoods built next to airports.

This is the same with major roads and interstates. The closer your property of interest is to a major highway, the more you must adjust your comp. Is the front door, back door, or side door next to a major road? This is the traffic rule, where a high level of traffic might be a deterrent for some buyers or potential homeowners. The same is true when it comes to the distance of certain commercial structures. In Tucson, one of the oldest shopping malls is the El Con Center (El Con Mall to locals), which was opened in 1960. In the 1990s, a lot of the residents who lived near the mall complained about the increase in traffic and the ability for people to cut through the neighborhood in order to reach the mall. This is just one example where location is a factor in adjustments, but there are others. Neighborhoods and cities change, as we've certainly seen, so what was a single-family inlet in the '60s is now the home of the local high school, the movie theater, or the mall.

I can't stress enough how important it is to learn and follow these rules. These are the rules that most of your buyers will follow, plain and simple. Knowing how to comp properties is what separates good wholesalers from great wholesalers; being able to accurately evaluate a property makes you indispensable to investors, other wholesalers, fix-and-flippers, or real estate agents in your area. You will also find those deals that other people often overlook.

I've been in this business for over twenty years and I still follow these appraisal rules, no matter the size or amount of the deal that I'm working on. I find these to be so important and a crucial part of understanding the ins and outs of business that I give them away. Not only do I post them on my Instagram page but I also host a weekly podcast about them. You can learn more about these appraisal rules by getting your appraiser's license (in Arizona, it takes seventy-five hours of education and costs $400; requirements and cost vary by state). You can research appraisal rules online, but, like my warning from earlier in the book, beware that not all online information is complete. Once you start to understand the appraisal rules and how they affect your comps, there are resources you can use to determine value without extensive research or additional education, and the best part is they're free.

How to Comp Like a Pro

One of the best and fastest ways to comp a property is by using the free Zillow app and website. Zillow is the leading real estate and rental marketplace, and it provides data and information on properties in various locations. Zillow showcases housing prices for homes that have been sold, those that are currently on the market, and even rentals; this information comes from the MLS, which means that it can show new homes that have gone on the market. Many sellers and agents and wholesalers use sites like Zillow or Opendoor to find out the worth of homes; the advantage is seeing what price point other homes have sold for. Zillow also gives us the opportunity to look at our subject property.

The disadvantage, as I noted earlier, especially for homeowners, is that Zillow doesn't account for any necessary repairs or renovations.

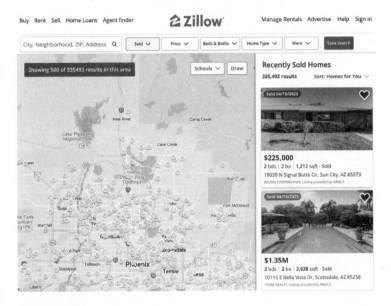

On both the app and the website, you can filter results to find the exact type of property you're looking for. Let's use the example from above. One property is:

- Single story.
- Three bedroom.
- Two bathroom.
- House was 1,765 square feet.
- Two-car garage and a pool.
- Lot size of 3,200 square feet.

The screenshot shows the filters I applied to find this type of home in the area of Phoenix:

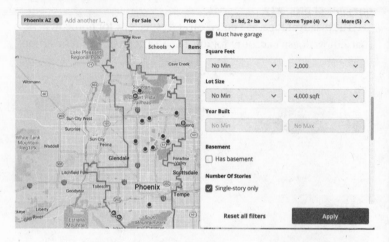

With these filters in place, we can see there are fifteen listings from agents and one listing from a homeowner. This is, of course, only an example, but you can see how easy it is to find similar properties. Zillow is a great resource to help you determine these numbers, but over time these calculations will start to come more naturally to you. I did a comp in ten minutes while sitting on my couch with a broken foot … but it took me years of deals and thousands of calculations to get to that point.

After you understand the basics of comping, then you can start using the numbers to figure out the value of a potential property (covered in detail in the next chapter).

WHOLESALE SUCCESS STORY
One Relationship Worth Thousands with Tabitha Jones

In January 2023 (a few short months ago), I reached out to a Realtor named James, marking the beginning of a transformative journey. James expressed interest in my wholesaling needs and wanted to set up a phone conversation. This conversation would set the stage for a fruitful collaboration.

I shared my goal with James, which was to find a distressed or original-condition property that we could transform into a beautiful home. Over a quick eight-minute chat, James presented two potential properties worth exploring. Among them was a home that had lingered on the market for over 100 days, priced at $699,000, with no offers on the table. James expressed the seller's need and motivation to sell the property. It was her childhood home, and she was ready to start a future in a new home.

I quickly conducted an analysis of the property. The closest comp (directly across the street) had recently been beautifully remodeled and was pending sale at $875,000 after just ten days on the market. Armed with this data, I ran my numbers and made an all-cash, quick-close offer for $540,000. After some negotiation, we agreed on the price, but we extended the closing period to accommodate the seller's needs. Once the contract was secured, I began looking to sell my equitable rights to my cash buyer network. Among the interested parties was a buyer I'd had previous business with who showed genuine interest and visited the property with James.

After my cash buyer did his due diligence, he offered $540,000 for the home. To turn a profit, I needed to renegotiate the price. Returning to James, I proposed acquiring the property for $500,000, aiming to anchor the negotiation lower than expected. To my surprise, the seller agreed to the new price and was ready to finish the sale of her home!

With the contract assigned to my cash buyer at $540,000 and with the seller and I agreeing to $500,000, we were headed to the closing table. Over a month later, the transaction concluded, and $40,000 was wired to my bank account—a testament to the financial gains achieved through just one healthy real estate agent relationship!

Beyond the monetary success, this transaction marked the birth of an invaluable relationship with James. Recognizing my integrity, transparency, and ability to close a challenging deal, he continues to involve me in opportunities that require cash offers or distressed properties.

The power of building strong relationships cannot be underestimated. Growing connections based on trust, collaboration, and mutual benefit can yield remarkable results. By nurturing even a single partnership, I not only achieved substantial financial gains but also laid a solid foundation for the continued growth and success of my business. Remember, success often relies on hard work and on the power of meaningful connections.

Embrace the potential that lies within building strong relationships, and watch as your business flourishes and exceeds your wildest expectations!

A QUICK RECAP

- Comping is the art of comparing aspects of a subject house or property to similar homes or properties in the same location by using historical sales data to help determine value.
- Comping uses apples-to-apples comparisons. You cannot, for instance, use a single-story property as a comparable to a two-story property.
- Appraisers use appraisal rules when assigning value to properties or to property characteristics. Wholesalers need to follow these rules to ensure we're also comparing apples to apples as much as possible.
- Software tools and websites can help wholesalers find comparable houses. (I mentioned in Chapter 5 that I use Privy and BatchLeads, which have fees, but you can also use free sites such as Zillow to find comparable properties.)

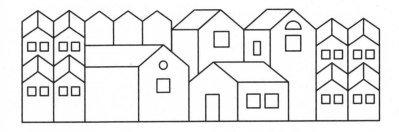

CHAPTER 7
Finding Your Wholesale Numbers

In the last chapter we looked at how to compare a subject property against comparables with similar characteristics to find the most accurate estimate of our property's potential value. Comping is a fundamental element to becoming a successful wholesaler. However, it's not the only metric that good wholesalers need to understand for assessing the viability of a deal. In this chapter, we look at the math that goes into a deal to understand the variables we must pay attention to, so we can determine value. Let's begin by looking at key terms for those variables.

Know Your Lingo

You've learned quite a bit of terminology throughout this book, but these are some of the most important terms and abbreviations you'll use when speaking with buyers, sellers, agents, and other investors:

- After repair value (ARV)
- Rehab costs
- Maximum allowable offer (MAO)

After Repair Value

The ARV is what a house is worth after it has been completely remodeled to the highest degree suitable to the area. The ARV of a property is what we as wholesalers concentrate on when it comes to determining the highest and best potential value for a property. As noted earlier in the book, ARV has been described as the wholesaler's North Star. The ARV is determined by:

- The highest and best use of a property.
- Sales of improved properties subject to adjustments and parameters found on the appraisal rules.

ARV is dependent on full-fledged improvements, so it's critical to understand how much the improvements or rehab will cost to get your property into this condition.

Rehab Costs

These costs are the renovation or repair expenses needed to bring a property up to a higher standard of condition. This covers everything from structural repairs to cosmetic updates, and these expenses vary by market. For example, renovating two similar homes, one in Phoenix and the other in Los Angeles, could have a 20 percent variance in cost. It's important to know these differences when buying properties in markets outside of where you live. Using a rehab estimator will give you the most accurate results, so I highly recommend finding one you like. Members of the BiggerPockets community have access to a rehab estimator that takes into consideration regional differences in price. You can find it at www.biggerpockets.com/rehab-estimator.

On the A&E show *Triple Digit Flip*, my cohosts and I discuss what we can do to elevate a property to retail standards. Sometimes this includes costly structural and design elements, sometimes less expensive improvements that deliver a big wow factor. Since rehabbing can involve a significant investment of time and money, you must always calculate what those expenses will be. Even if you're not renovating the property yourself, it's important to understand these expenses so you can accurately relay them to a potential buyer. A costly error new wholesalers make is not taking into account rehab expenses when calculating how much to offer for a property. If you don't factor in these costs correctly, you run the risk of overpaying for your contract. This might result in buyers passing on the deal, so you'll need to renegotiate or cancel the contract with the seller. That feeds the vicious cycle of wholesaler distrust. Agents and sellers detest wasted time much more than realistic yet low offers. So, how do you effectively calculate these rehab or renovation costs?

Determine the Scope of Work

The first step is to figure out the type of damage, if any, there is to a property. Asking detailed questions prior to contracting the home is essential in making sure your offer price is reflective of all the variables. Sellers are required to reveal any material defects in property disclosures; however, I've rarely had a seller reveal everything. That's why it's better to be liberal with your numbers than try to force a deal. I recommend hiring your own independent inspector to run an assessment, who might find damages or problems you wouldn't otherwise know about or that the seller is concealing or may not be aware of. Plus, an inspection report gives you a written record of items you can leverage to negotiate price. It's wiser to be aware of issues ahead of time than stuck with a contract you can't sell.

Estimate Labor Costs

When estimating labor costs, you need to account for how pricing varies by contractor ability and geographical region. A contractor's skill level is highly subjective and can drastically increase the expense depending on the job. While your buyer will be making these improvements, what we assume to be a complete remodel, wholesalers need to know what these costs might be. For example, a Level 5 drywall finish requires more skill than an average drywall contractor has. What about the cost of paint? I can now look at a wall and mentally estimate the time and labor prep, but it took years of experience. It's also important to note that the type of project requires different levels of finish with varying price points. This is where your research is crucial. You need an accurate estimate to not end up pricing the cost of the house higher than necessary.

Before all this, though, ask the seller or seller's representative to send you detailed pictures and a written description of the condition of the property before going under contract. If you have a contractor in mind, invite them to view the property with you, so they can make estimates. While you can hire a contractor specifically for a bid, particularly somebody you trust who you've worked with in the past, be careful not to misuse a contractor for estimates if you don't intend to hire them.

Every buyer will have their own network of contractors. For example, I have one buyer who only buys fire-burned properties. Every time I get an estimate from a contractor on how much repairs will cost, my budget is 20 percent to 25 percent higher than this buyer's. I could never understand how he was making these deals work until I did a site visit one day and saw that he and his family were doing all the work themselves.

You want to understand costs so it guides your offer but not be used as a representation of the total costs. The last thing you want is a situation where a renovation is more expensive than originally anticipated and your buyer gets upset after the fact at the dollar amount you provided.

Once you have all your estimates, add up the costs for materials and labor to get an idea of the full scope of the renovation from start to finish.

Maximum Allowable Offer

The maximum allowable offer, or MAO, is the highest purchase amount an investor can offer on a house while still making a reasonable profit. This means knowing how much you can afford to offer for a property, so you don't end up overbidding, which might lead to a renegotiation or a cancellation of contract. Now, "reasonable profit" is wholly dependent on what you're looking to make from a deal, making this a subjective variable. Every investor has their own threshold for profit margin. My approach is to offer a seller as much money as possible while still making a profit margin relative to the value I created with my work. The calculations for MAO are related to your calculations for the maximum potential value of the property, or the ARV.

Putting It All Together

Now you know the important terminology in determining the potential value of a property, but how the heck do you calculate it? The process of finding and evaluating a property is pretty straightforward:

- You find a distressed property primed for a great deal.
- You find a relevant comp in the area.
- You calculate the ARV costs.
- You include your estimated rehab costs within ARV potential.
- You find your MAO to understand what you should offer on the original distressed property.

You might be thinking, "Jamil, that's certainly easy for you!"

You're right. I've been at this for a long time, but it's not as complicated as you might think. You can use different formulas when calculating MAO, but in the simplest terms, your MAO is the amount you want to offer after the ARV has been set and you have your rehab estimate. This is a book to get you started on the path to being a wholesaler, so I'll explain how to find an MAO and ARV as a wholesaler.

There are three ways to calculate the wholesaler's maximum allowable offer (WMAO):

- Fix & Flip MAO formula.
- Flat Percentage of ARV (Standard).
- Flat Percentage of ARV (Regional). This is the method I use.

Get ready for more acronyms and some math. These formulas might make you feel as though you walked into a calculus class by mistake, but they're incredibly important to understand how to determine MAO.

Fix & Flip MAO Formula

$$\text{WMAO} =$$

ARV − Initial closing costs − Resale closing costs − Commissions − Holding costs − Rehab budget − HML/PML costs* − Hazard insurance* − Fix-and-flipper profits − Wholesaler profits

*(if applicable)

That is a lot, I know, so let's break this down:
- WMAO is the wholesaler's maximum allowable offer.
- ARV is the amount you believe the home or property will sell for after all repairs or renovations.
- Initial purchase closing costs and resale closing costs are the expenses in the process of transferring ownership of the property (e.g., initial cost of the property, title insurance, appraisals/inspections, document fees).
- Commissions go to anyone involved in the sale (e.g., real estate agent).
- Holding costs and fees are the taxes, insurance, HOA fees, etc.
- The rehab budget is the estimated amount for renovations.
- HML/PML costs are fees that have been applied by your hard money lender (HML) or private money lender (PML) (discussed in detail in Chapter 9).
- Hazard insurance includes any maintenance that needs to be done (e.g., lawn maintenance, plumbing, electrical) and any utilities that need to be paid (e.g., electric, water, trash).

- Profits made by the fix-and-flipper (the buyer) and the wholesaler.

Now, with all of these expenses, you may think you need to offer a low price on the property to the seller to increase the profit margins on your deal with the buyer. Don't. A good wholesaler, which is what I want you to be, will pay 100 percent of what the property is worth in its as-is current condition. Period. Good wholesalers don't lowball anyone. If the margins look too slim after your calculations, then consider passing this offer on to someone in your network. That's why we do these types of calculations. It's not only to understand what you can afford to offer and what you might potentially earn but also to decide if the deal is right for you in the first place.

Flat Percentage of ARV (Standard)

This formula is far simpler yet it still delivers a reliable offer point:

WMAO = ARV x 70% – Rehab budget – Wholesale fee

- Multiply the ARV by 70% (to insulate for extra expenses).
- Subtract both the rehab budget and the wholesale fee that you hope to make.

Let's say that the ARV for the property is $170,000. Take that amount and multiply it by 70 percent, then subtract the rehab costs and your fee. Let's say in this case the former is $30,000 and the latter is $10,000.

The example formula is:

WMAO = $170,000 x 0.70 – $30,000 – $10,000

The WMAO would be $79,000. That might be lower than a seller would like, and it doesn't take into consideration markets that are more competitive. In markets with high appreciation and high demand, you'll need to offer more money because of competition from others interested in this property.

Flat Percentage of ARV (Regional)

This formula is considered the easiest to calculate and remember, making it a favorite of many wholesalers. It still uses the flat percentage from the previous strategy, but here you'll use a regionally specific percentage. In the example below, I use Phoenix's ARV percentage of 70 percent for cosmetic remodels. For a full gut remodel, you'd subtract 20 percent to accommodate for the expenses, so you'd use 50% of ARV. Let's say the ARV is $185,000.

$$WMAO = ARV \times \%$$

Cosmetic Remodel:

WMAO = $185,000 x 0.70 (70%)

That makes the WMAO $129,500.

Full-Gut Remodel:

WMAO = $185,000 x 0.50 (50%)

That makes the WMAO $92,500.

When calculating WMAO, I prefer a regionally specific flat percentage of ARV because it's dependent on the property's condition. For example, a 1,300-square-foot full-gut remodel will have a different ARV in Mobile, Alabama, than in Boston, Massachusetts.

This is my preferred method for a few reasons:

- It's fast.
- It's easy to calculate.
- It's easy to adjust between the two.
- There's no need to know a rehab budget—just if it's a full-gut or cosmetic job. Pictures will tell you all that you need to know.

Now you know how to find properties, determine their ARV, and figure out your MAO for your desired profit margin. In the next chapter, I'll discuss how to convert your leads into contracts.

A QUICK RECAP

- ARV is what a property is worth after it has been remodeled to the highest degree suitable to the area surrounding it.
- Renovation is the process of bringing a property up to a higher standard of condition.
- MAO is the highest purchase amount that an investor can offer on a property while still making their desired profit.
- There are three formulas to determine your WMAO. I prefer multiplying the ARV against your city's flat ARV percentage.
- A flat percentage helps you calculate your MAO. This percentage is based on the demand and appreciation of the area's market:
  - In a low-demand, low-appreciation market, the flat percentage may be lower, such as 50 percent for a cosmetic fix and 30 percent for full-gut reno.
  - In a high-demand, high-appreciation market, the flat percentage will be higher; for example, 80 percent for cosmetic and 60 percent for full-gut.

Scaling a Wholesaling Empire

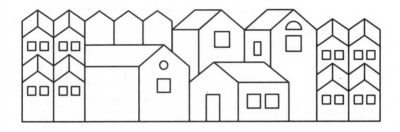

CHAPTER 8
Dispo(sition) Inferno

Disposition wholesalers: my favorite subject! So, what is disposition? Disposition is the art of selling. We call it an art because you have to understand how to find buyers, create financial opportunities for these buyers, and then see that the deals get closed. This requires a tremendous amount of research, knowledge, technique, and skill. I mentioned earlier in the book that one of the largest issues in the wholesale industry is deals getting canceled due to the inability of acquisition wholesalers to find buyers and complete transactions. If an acquisition wholesaler doesn't have their own funds, it's important that they partner with a company that does. KeyGlee offers a solution by financially backstopping our joint venture partners (discussed in Chapter 9) and building relationships with other buyers to help acquisition wholesalers write offers and find buyers for their contracts.

There's a misconception that dispositions need to be handled by the original contract holder (that is, the acquisitions wholesaler). A wholesaler can transfer their equitable interest to another wholesaler by way of an option agreement. (Don't worry if this isn't clear right now. The next chapter is all about types of contracts.) When a wholesaler transfers their equitable interest to a disposition wholesaler, they are leveraging an entire network of cash buyers, and this is tremendously helpful in getting deals done. Alternatively, wholesalers who have their own funds and networks may decide to handle dispositions on their own. For new wholesalers, partnering with or forming a close relationship with your buyer is the fastest way to legitimize yourself as a wholesaler. Your buyer is typically the individual who is bringing money to the deal and writing the check to the seller. Because of this, not knowing what your buyers want is a cardinal sin in wholesaling.

The first decision to make is whether you want to handle dispositions yourself or if you want to partner with a disposition wholesaler.

WHAT IS A DISPOSITION WHOLESALER?

A disposition wholesaler is an expert in the business of creative buyer relationships. They exist in every major real estate market, are financially capable of closing, and usually carry the necessary licensing to negotiate contracts on someone else's behalf. Some of the larger companies in this space are KeyGlee, HomeVestors, NetWorth Realty, and New Western Acquisitions. I've worked with great people from all of these organizations. The primary focus of a disposition wholesaler is finding buyers, building relationships, and curating property opportunities. Many acquisition wholesalers would rather focus on their core business model than invest the time, energy, and money required to find the perfect buyer for their property. Disposition wholesalers are valuable because we find qualified buyers for acquisition wholesalers and we're a single resource for purchase opportunities for buyers. Like with everything else, the fastest way to find disposition wholesalers is to do an internet search using the terms "cash homebuyer" and your preferred city or location.

You might be thinking, "Wait a minute, Jamil, that's looking for a homebuyer. How will that help me with my dispositions? I don't want to actually buy a home."

That's because in wholesaling every buyer is also a seller. Wholesalers constantly work to increase our visibility through advertising to attract homeowners and build relationships with buyers. When I first started as a wholesaler, I scaled my business rapidly by partnering with a disposition wholesaler. I spent my time and energy finding and locking up deals with sellers and then optioned these deals to my dispo wholesaler to sell for me. This allowed me to focus my time and energy on what I did best: acquisitions. We created a mutually beneficial relationship where we both made money and the buyers and sellers got what they wanted. I strengthened my focus on my acquisitions model, allowing me to build relationships with real estate agents and wholesalers while keeping my promises that deals would not fall through. My offers were financially backed by my disposition partner, so any time we needed to close on a deal, we could. My reputation in Phoenix as a successful wholesaler grew rapidly, and more opportunities came my way by word of mouth.

Some reader might think, "But Jamil, you're leaving money on the table. Bringing in a dispo wholesaler on the deal gives them a piece of the pie." That's true, but they may also sell for a higher price than I could because they have eager buyers in the wings.

Here's an example of when I acted as the dispositions wholesaler in a deal and generated higher profits for an acquisitions wholesaler than he could have on his own, making a profit for us both. He brought me a deal and was seeking $60,000 to sell this particular contract. After analyzing the numbers, I said I'd be the buyer. Not long after this, he questioned how much I intended to sell the property for, likely trying to understand what type of profit I was seeking.

After discussing what he wanted to get out of the deal, we decided that we could benefit mutually if we did a joint venture (JV) partnership in which we split the profits 50/50. At this point, he disclosed that his original contract price for the property was $50,000. I knew that I could sell the contract for this property for $100,000, so instead of him only making $10,000 by selling to me at $60,000, we were each able to make $25,000 by selling the contract to my buyer. We JV'd the deal and both made money. The point of this story is that he brought my attention to a property I wouldn't have known about, and he didn't know the true value of the property. This success led to a long-term partnership in which we do a lot of deals together.

If you can build relationships with disposition wholesalers, you free yourself up to focus on the acquisition side of the business. Conversely, as a disposition wholesaler, relationships with acquisition wholesalers brings you deals you wouldn't otherwise know about. The moral of this story is that business is about relationships.

How Dispositions Work

I'll give a caveat about finding cash buyers through an internet search: It can be tedious and time-consuming. Cash buying is identifiable through:

- Tax records.
- MLS listing history.
- Rental websites.
- Social media posts.
- Deeds of trust.

Let's go into some detail about each of these.

Tax Records

Every state keeps records of the legal property owners for all property within the state, with the chain of ownership traced for decades. Oftentimes, these records indicate whether a buyer paid cash for the property or financed it. If the former, this might indicate these buyers are in the business of buying and selling property and perhaps interested in purchasing your potential future deals. Tax records are also useful to trace wholesaler activity. If a property was bought and sold by way of double escrow or transactional funding, the original wholesaler will show up on the tax record. Double escrow is a set of real estate transactions involving two contracts of sale for the same property, two different back-to-back buyers, at the same or two different prices, arranged to close on the same date. Transactional funding is a type of real estate loan that allows you to buy and sell real estate using the same funding source. I continue to build my list of cash buyers and wholesalers by reviewing Arizona's tax records every month for new cash or hard money financed transactions.

MLS Listing History

Listings are another great resource for finding cash buyers. When a rehabber or fix-and-flipper renovates a home, they typically sell that property on the MLS. Every morning, I check for properties that were listed the night prior that look renovated, with photos of closets with no clothes in them, and owned by an LLC entity. Clothes in the closet, or lack of them, tell me whether someone still lives at the property. I look for properties that have been recently flipped, check who the owner of that property is, skip-trace their contact information, and reach out to determine if they're interested in doing business with me. This strategy allows me to time when I reach out to potential buyers. Someone who has just recently listed their flipped property is more receptive to purchasing their next flip. This isn't limited to fix-and-flippers; you can also find the real estate agents who list these properties because they have relationships with cash buyers who are in the business of flipping. Real estate agents often specialize in types of properties, and an agent who works with one investor is likely to work with many.

Rental Websites

Rental websites, like Zillow, are sources for finding viable buy-and-hold investors (as the name indicates, they are the opposite of fix-and-flippers). For an area where you want to find a potential deal, you can go to Zillow to see a listing of all the properties for rent in and around that area. With a property address, you can then research who the owner of the property is via state tax records. Many buy-and-hold investors like to buy properties in close proximity for ease and convenience of management. Don't worry if the listings are managed by a property manager or a real estate agent. Remember, real estate agents love opportunities to sell to their cash-buying clients; meanwhile, property managers are incentivized to increase the size of their clients' portfolios, so they too may be helpful in connecting you to their clients. This could means sales for the real estate agent or the property manager, making this also an opportune avenue to develop relationships and networks.

Social Media Posts

In today's world, people love to share what they're doing on social media. I have found many cash buyers on Facebook, Instagram, and LinkedIn, and on sites like BiggerPockets. In the following image, you can see the tabs with the tools and forums offered to members on the BiggerPockets site.

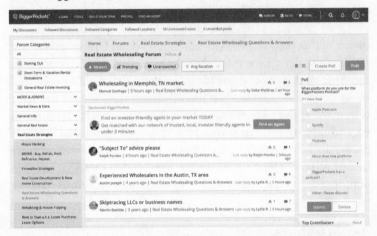

Social media and member sites like BiggerPockets allow you to create relationships and send outreach messages at scale. Remember to read and follow community guidelines so as not to get marked as a spammer. When building a business around wholesaling, social media will be a lucrative resource for finding and building relationships with cash buyers because many commenters make recommendations of cash buyers known to them. Another avenue is through in-person networking events and meetups, as discussed earlier in the book. After the isolation caused by COVID-19, many real estate investors are now actively attending live events. Never underestimate the power of attending in person. This is how you can best start creating relationships. Over time, you'll build rapport and find opportunities together for both current cash buyers and potential deals.

Deeds of Trust

A deed of trust is a document that can be used in financed real estate transactions instead of a mortgage. A deed transfers the legal title or property to a third party, such as a bank, private lender, or other financial institution, to hold until the borrower repays their debt to the lender. Deeds of trust are recorded against properties and, in many cases, are public record. Wholesalers can search public records to determine the owner or who lent on a property. Using a deed of trust isn't as common today as it was even a few years ago, but some states require them. They are:

- Alaska
- Arizona
- California
- Colorado
- Idaho
- Illinois
- Mississippi
- Missouri
- Montana
- North Carolina
- Tennessee
- Texas
- Virginia
- West Virginia

Best Prospecting Methods for Dispositions

Dispositions are probably better suited for people who feel more comfortable behind the scenes. If you're considering being an acquisitions wholesaler, then consider using SMS/texting; if dispositions sound more interesting, then you're better off using email blasts. I've found these to be great avenues as a way to get the attention of a larger audience.

Let's start with acquisition wholesaling. I'm sure I don't have to tell you about the power of texting:

- 98 percent of U.S. adults own mobile phones.

- 95 percent of text messages are responded to within three minutes of receipt.
- 48 percent of consumers prefer direct communication from brands via SMS.
- 90 percent of customers prefer text messages over direct phone calls.
- 8.2 billion people worldwide use mobile phones.
- Real estate is the top industry using SMS.

Texting has become popular across industries and age ranges, with fast speed and ease of use, and more people respond to a text than a phone call. Many people don't realize that they can use texting to reach a large audience, plus it's quite economical. There are a lot of obvious benefits for wholesalers, such as effectively organizing your text conversations and responses.

Here are some of the basics of SMS outreach that I teach my students:

- Select your target market.
- Get a list of contacts for that market from a list provider (Batch-Leads, PropStream, Privy, etc.; see Chapter 5).
- Skip-trace that list.
- Scrub the list, meaning check it against Do Not Call lists.[3]
- Import that list into a software program (such as BatchLeads).
- Send an SMS blast to the list.
- Use a conversational tone in your script.

Some of the lead lists that you use will include distressed properties or situations, which are, of course, the opportunities that we look for as acquisition wholesalers.

Email Blasts

For disposition wholesalers, there is also the option of sending out email blasts. Email blasts enable you to send out a single message to a large list, but you should use a third-party email marketing automation service, which is a service that sends out large batches of emails.

---

3 www.donotcall.gov

One of the more popular of these is Mailchimp. Other well-known services include:

- Constant Contact.
- HubSpot.
- Infusionsoft (now known as Keap).
- ActiveCampaign.
- Drip.
- Omnisend.
- Close.

This is in no way a complete list, so if you have a service you use for your other business (if you have one), then definitely use that service. If not, many of these platforms offer free trials, so play around to see which one feels easiest to you. You'll want to use a headline that teases the most attractive characteristics of a property and creates a sense of urgency, but you also don't want it to be too long.

Some good headlines in the Phoenix area might be:

- 3 New Deals! GCU down the street!
- Easy West Side Flip
- Phoenix Off-Market Flip ($25K)
- New Tempe Duplex (Close to ASU Tempe)

In these examples, the location of the property is in the headline. Another thing to consider is the day and time when you have the blast sent out. Now, you might not think that's important, but it is. You want to send it when people are most likely to open your email and respond. In our industry, the highest rate of open is Mondays between 6 p.m. and 7 p.m. Your day and time may be different. Some email providers or services may offer recommended times to send or schedule your emails on their platforms for the maximum open rate.

When possible, send out one property per email to avoid receivers being overwhelmed or confused. Occasionally, having more than one property in an email can be beneficial, depending on the property (such as two properties on the same street). Importantly, ensure that you're describing the property accurately. Remember: Accuracy matters to potential buyers so they don't waste their time and get annoyed with you.

- Show the entire front of the house.
- Show any parking (garage, carport, etc.).
- Include Google Street View images.
- Show interior images of all rooms, including any damage.
- For condos, show the outside of the whole complex and any amenities (e.g., laundry room, pool and fitness areas).

Last, use your full name or the name of your company in your sign-off, and always include an option for recipients to opt out of emails. Similar to the Telephone Consumer Protection Act discussed in Chapter 5, the CAN-SPAM Act[4] sets the rules for commercial email. CAN-SPAM establishes requirements for message frequency and gives recipients the right to opt out of emails.

Following Up

I can't stress this enough: One of the most important steps for wholesalers is following up. If someone contacted you as a buyer, follow up via text or email, however you originally sent the message, to determine if a property works for them.

I talked about how speed is crucial when sellers contact you, but it's even more important with interested buyers. I've had plenty of instances in which a buyer expressed interest in a property, but because of a delay in my response, they moved forward with a different purchase and different wholesaler. When a buyer's hot, they're hot, and you have minutes to strike. Cultivate that interest, and if you have enough demand for your deal, you can create scarcity. There's nothing better than having two buyers who want your deal, but instead of creating a bidding war, have them race to title. The first one with an earnest money deposit receipt (that is, has the down payment ready to go) gets the house. While I'm on the subject, let me talk a little bit about bidding wars with your wholesale buyers. There are differing schools of thought on this concept, but after selling over

---

4   Controlling the Assault of Non-Solicited Pornography and Marketing Act of 2003.

6,000 deals, I can assure you that bidding wars are a bad idea. Think about it. Your buyers spent time driving to the property, running their numbers, making a mental commitment, only to hear that you changed the goalposts and now want a highest and best offer and won't accept a contract until the end of the day. Sure, you might sell this house for a little more this time, but I can promise you that you've angered every other buyer who didn't get it. And they could be your connection to other sales. I train my buyers to act fast and commit to deals quickly rather than look like unreliable sources of deals. With that said, if I expect them to act fast and commit quickly, then I had better do so in my responses as well.

Remember the case study from Chapter 5 with Andy and Albaro? The secret ingredient to that deal was Albaro's dedication to following up with both his real estate agent and Andy. Follow-up is so important because it shows your buyers that you care about their situation and want to find a good deal for them. It also shows that you know how to manage your business and time, which are promising characteristics for potential business associates. Agents or other wholesalers will sometimes contact a buyer only to ghost them. We all know how that feels. Good wholesalers always follow up with their contacts, whether that's a seller, buyer, other wholesaler, real estate agent, or someone else. Make sure that you stay aware of their current situation. If Albaro hadn't followed up with his agent, he never would have known that the seller needed a solution that luckily we could provide. Follow up your emails, texts, phone calls, and any other form of contact. Even if your buyers and sellers decide not to move forward at this point, or they decide to go in a different direction, follow up with them at a later date. Check in to see how things worked out. Even if you weren't on a deal, they will remember how you handled their situation and might recommend you to others.

How to Choose Your Focus: Disposition or Acquisition?

Now that you understand acquisitions and dispositions, you might be asking which one might be right for you. Or do you need to choose at all?

Yes. Choosing a focus in wholesaling is really important. It's rare to find a unicorn wholesaler who is talented in all aspects of the business. And that's true for every field, even outside of real estate. For me, I'm more talented as an acquisitions wholesaler because my ability and skills to connect and build relationships with agents and other wholesalers is what has brought me my success. With that said, if I hadn't focused on building great buyer relationships, I wouldn't be where I am today. It's not that I couldn't have focused instead on disposition wholesaling, but I spent much of my early career building acquisition relationships. I couldn't do both equally well. Josiah Grimes and Hunter Runyon, co-founders of KeyGlee, are more proficient than me at disposition-focused infrastructures. They are extremely talented at seeking and finding new buyer relationships, building databases, and crafting communication tools that then are used to disseminate my deals to thousands of buyers rapidly for fast sales and smooth transaction processes. I'm more gregarious and good at relationship-building; I'm not talented at building out systems and technical infrastructure. Hunter, by comparison, is shyer, so he sold his first fifty deals without making a single phone call. That's absolute talent.

When deciding on whether to focus on acquisitions or dispositions, it's important that you determine what type of investor you are. Being an acquisition wholesaler requires strong interpersonal skills and emotional intelligence. Disposition wholesalers, on the other hand, must know how to effectively communicate information to large numbers of people. Many of our buyers exchange few words with us when committing to a wholesale purchase; that was how Hunter sold so many houses without calling anyone. This shows that there are many ways to excel as a wholesaler, regardless of your personality type. When considering where you fit in best, let self-awareness be your guide. Make a list of pros and cons, such as the following:

Some PROS of pursuing disposition wholesaling:

- You have no marketing expenses.
- The money is available when you begin work on a deal.

- You have quick turnaround on deals.
- You create long-term relationships.

Some CONS of disposition are:
- You don't control the deal.
- Deals are subject to the terms of an existing contract.
- You have a smaller spread.
- You may have to babysit the buyers to get to close.

Now that you have an understanding of disposition and acquisition wholesaling, I'll get to the hallmark of our business in the next chapter: signing on the dotted line.

WHOLESALE SUCCESS STORY
Embracing Collaboration with Jonah Korchin

"It's better to have half a watermelon than the entirety of a grape."
– Max Maxwell

Real estate investing can have a bad reputation for being a cutthroat industry. But the most successful entrepreneurs understand that it's through *collaboration* that you make the most money! I'm Jonah Korchin, an investor and wholesaler in Northern California and Colorado. I do my business exclusively through agent acquisitions and rely on solid disposition wholesalers to find buyers for all my deals. This allows me to focus on what I'm good at and not waste time trying to dispo deals. It's a symbiotic relationship! Here's the story of my journey, where I learned to embrace the power of joint venturing with my competition.

My true strength has always been acquisitions. I love talking to real estate agents, schmoozing, and getting them to love me back and give me exclusive off-market deals. I realized that as I scaled, I would rather focus on my expertise than attempt things I'm not good at—including dispositions. I did okay when I tried to dispo all my own deals, but not nearly as good as I would have wanted. Once I focused solely on agent acquisitions, I was able to scale from two markets to four within three months! This was possible because I squadded up with an amazing disposition wholesaler who (1) knew the market, (2) had hundreds of buyers, and (3) could give me a solid buy number. I just had to copy and paste the acquisition system into different markets! I'm planning on opening up in Southern California within three months—if I'd tried to tackle every aspect of the process myself, it would have taken me years to gain the knowledge of how each specific market worked. This strategic approach allowed me to leverage my expertise in marketing, negotiation, and property sales, enabling me to maximize my profits and streamline the wholesaling process.

This journey of joint venturing with disposition wholesalers illuminates the incredible, transformative power of collaboration. Since this shift to focusing on my strengths, I'm on track to run a $625,000-per-year business. By embracing the power of partnerships, I unleashed an unstoppable force of efficiency, paving the way for an abundance of lucrative deals. Furthermore, my network has flourished, fortified by the strong bond of collaboration as I harnessed the diverse expertise and complementary roles of my joint venture partners in the wholesale process.

Key takeaway? Specialize as much as possible, and find partners to do everything that you are bad at. Don't do every part of the process—just the parts you're best at!

A QUICK RECAP

- Disposition is the art of selling: understanding how to find opportunities and getting a deal closed for your buyer. This requires research, knowledge, technique, and skill.
- Researching includes finding deeds of trust and state tax records (etc.) and searching rental websites and the MLS (etc.).
- Don't create bidding wars. Instead encourage multiple buyers to be the first to take title.
- Follow up with your buyers quickly and consistently via text, email, or phone calls. Even if you aren't working on a current deal together, strong follow-up habits might result in future deals.

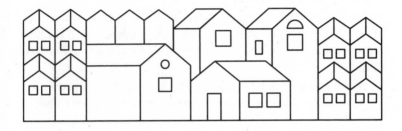

CHAPTER 9
Signing on the Dotted Line

In the previous chapters, you learned what wholesaling is; how to find deals and find buyers; how to establish value; and how to understand the costs of a deal. Now it's time to learn how to put all that information into a contract. This chapter is about understanding how to put together this final essential piece, which allows us to finalize our deal and make some money from it. I know the prospect of a contract sounds daunting, but it's part of ensuring that you've done everything necessary and haven't forgotten anything. There are five types of contracts wholesalers use, depending on the deal:

- A-B contract.
- Option agreement contract.
- Assignment contract.
- B-C contract.
- Joint venture (JV) contract.

Not only will we look at each of these in depth but also the circumstances in which you'd want to use each one. Let's start with the standard A-B contract.

What Is an A-B Contract?

An A-B contract is between the seller (Person A) and wholesaler (Person B); it opens up the first escrow on a property. This is the first leg of a wholesale transaction. Here are some reasons to use A-B contracts:

- Secures wholesaler's right to purchase a subject property.
- Establishes wholesaler's equitable interest in the subject property.
- Protects both buyer and seller by clearly describing the rights and responsibilities of each party.
- Establishes timelines for the different milestones within a deal, such as inspections, financing, performance/closing, etc.
- Clearly discloses wholesaler's intent to resell for profit and any potential conflicts.

At the end of the day, we want contracts to be fair to both parties, so everyone has equal footing during the process. The A-B contract can be broken down into two types: the standard Realtor Association A-B contract and the Custom A-B contract.

Realtor Association A-B Contract

Realtor Association A-B contracts are used by the Board of Realtors (that is, the National Association of Realtors®, or NAR). Because they are used by NAR, which is the leading real estate regulatory agency, these contracts are well trusted in the industry and accepted by all brokerages. Realtor Association A-B contracts, available only to Realtors, strive to protect both the buyer and the seller.

Custom A-B Contract

Custom A-B contracts are, as the name implies, customized for whatever is wanted in the deal. These are always written by attorneys.

They aren't as well known as the Realtor Association A-B contracts, but they are accepted by some brokerages (usually small to mid-size brokerages). Unlike the Realtor Association A-B contracts, anyone can use these contracts (including Realtors).

These custom contracts are not better or worse; custom contracts primarily address wholesaling points or situations that the Realtor Association A-B contract might not. While these two contracts have some differences, they also share common language that you'll find in most contracts of this nature:

- Purchase price.
- Earnest money deposit (EMD).
- Close of escrow (COE).
- Property title.
- Inspection period.
- Possession.
- Financing type.
- Cure period.
- Additional terms.

What do all these words mean?

Purchase Price

The purchase price is the agreed-upon amount between the seller and buyer for the purchase of the property. This is the amount a buyer is willing to pay for the subject property, and it might include closing costs or fees. For wholesalers, this price should equal the MAO, which we discussed in Chapter 7. The only instances in which these differ are if you miscalculated your MAO or when you or a buyer partner decide on a different use for the property.

Earnest Money Deposit

The EMD is a deposit made by the buyer as a show of good faith when making an offer on the subject property. It is also a form of legal consideration consummating the contract and demonstrates the buyer's commitment to follow through on the transaction. This amount can be a certain percentage of the total purchase price. Along with EMD, other terms are "good faith deposit" and "escrow deposit," because it's held in escrow by the chosen title company or by a real estate attorney. Because this is a sign of good faith on the buyer's side, if they decide to cancel the purchase within the contingency period, they're usually entitled to a return of their deposit. However, if the buyer backs out after the contingency period and there's no valid reason given, the seller is entitled to keep that money.

The inspection period can be a wholesaler's best friend and worst enemy. It's also the most abused buyer's right because the inability to sell a contract is not a valid reason to cancel the sale. When a wholesaler cancels because of an inability to sell a contract, it reduces the financial risk for the wholesaler because they get their EMD back but this also wastes the seller's time and is an invalid reason to cancel a purchase. Inspections are meant to determine property condition, not for marketing a contract. Hence the wholesaler paradox. No one wants either to buy a bad deal or get a reputation for cancelling contracts, but if you can't find any prospects to purchase your contract before your contingency period is up, doesn't that indicate it might actually be a bad deal after all? I've had many contracts that I was unable to sell during my inspection period, and I can't always say that it fared well for me because I had to cancel the contract. However, at the end of the day, my reputation is always worth more than making a bad investment.

I recognize that not everybody has the ability to make the same calls as I do. I'm not advocating that you shouldn't cancel and thus put yourself in a bad investment. But in an industry in which your reputation and network connections can make or break your business, these decisions matter. This is why knowing your numbers and being extraordinarily intentional about any deal is so important.

Close of Escrow (COE)

COE is usually the final step in the process of buying and selling the subject property. Escrow, as described above under EMD, is the legal arrangement in which a third party temporarily holds the buyer's good faith payment. COE is the point when the title company or real estate attorney receives the funds and documents from a lender for the purchase and holds them until the buyer and seller finalize the paperwork, including signing the purchase agreement. The seller is transferring their ownership of the property to the buyer, and the buyer is paying the remaining purchase price minus their earnest deposit amount. This completes all the paperwork and all the funds or fees are collected. The transaction is reviewed, and aside from any changes, the deal is recorded with the county and deemed complete. There's also the option to include a post-COE agreement, such as an extended possession by the previous owner, which I'll talk about later in this chapter.

Property Title

The title is a statement on who owns the property. You can think of it like the receipt at a grocery store; whether you bought your groceries with a credit card or cash, you're in possession of the food and the receipt. Even if you lose the receipt, you still own the groceries and the store has a record of your purchase. In this case, the grocery store functions like a title company, which is a business that specializes in title searches and insurance and has authority to amend records of ownership. Whenever a property is bought or sold, a title company does a search to determine the ownership of that property as well as identify any liens, fines, or impediments that might affect the transfer of ownership. Many real estate title companies are responsible for managing the process of escrow and transactional transfers.

Inspection Period

The inspection period is a contractual contingency that takes place within a previously agreed-upon timeframe between the parties of the contract, whereby a buyer may assess and evaluate the physical condition of the home. This is when an acquisitions wholesaler must correctly calculate any rehab estimates by investigating issues with the property that may not have been easily detected in photos or during an initial walkthrough or shared by the seller. This typically includes independent inspections by various trades such as electrical, plumbing, foundation, septic, and pest control contractors. The wholesaler pays for these inspections.

Possession

Possession is the term used to describe at what point a wholesaler and buyer will take possession of the property. Possession is an important part of the contract because every situation is different. For example, if a tenant still lives on the property or if the seller needs time to pack up their belongings before leaving the property, possession may not happen for a few days, a few weeks, or longer. Here's a sample of a contract KeyGlee worked on in which the buyer purchased the property while a tenant was still under their rental contract:

8. ADDITIONAL TERMS AND CONDITIONS

8a.	155	*Purchase of property in as-is condition*
	156	*Buyer will be assuming property with a*
	157	*month to month tenant in place. All security*
	158	*deposits that were given to seller by tenant*
	159	*shall be credited to Buyer at close of escrow*
	160	*as well as prorated rent*
	161	

As you see, the details of the possession were placed within the additional terms and conditions section of the contract, showing that a tenant already lives on the property in a month-by-month agreement, and the tenant's security deposit must be transferred to the buyer. This doesn't pertain only to a person; possessions can also be included, such as appliances, furniture, or other items belonging to the seller or tenant.

Financing Type

Financing type is how a buyer is paying for the property, which can be with cash or through a hard money lender or private money lender (and so on). For wholesalers, our buyers will most likely purchase a property with with cash or one of the following two options.

1. **Hard Money Lender:** A hard money lender (HML) is an asset-based loan or type of funding that provides financing

when a borrower (our buyer) receives funds for the purchase of real property. "Hard money" means that the financing is secured against a hard asset, which is the property itself or cross-collateralized against the borrower's other properties or assets, depending on the aggressiveness of the lender. HMLs are usually issued by private investors or companies and will generally consist of straight-line interest rates without any principal payments. This means for the borrower, their credit report isn't run when they apply for financing and their payments apply only toward the interest and not the actual principal. Now, before you get flashbacks from the predatory use of loans during the Great Recession (and earlier), let me explain how a borrower can get a loan without a credit check. HMLs are asset-based loans, meaning a financial institution loans money and secures that loan against the property as collateral. The borrower then signs a promissory note to pay back the hard money lender; however, since these are nonrecourse loans, they typically do not involve a personal guarantee, so if a deal goes wrong, no one can take the borrower's cars or other possessions not used as collateral. As a wholesaler, I use hard money when I need to close on a property before I resell it, and the majority of my buyers use hard money financing for their acquisition and construction costs. One of my earliest relationships as a wholesaler was with a hard money lender. A good deal becomes a great deal when you attach approved financing.

2. **Private Money Lender:** In many cases, a private money lender (PML) is someone known to the buyer, such as a friend or family member. They can also be private investors willing to loan money to buyers or other investors, usually using promissory notes as official instruments of security. Depending on the PML, they may run credit checks, though this is more likely when you're a stranger to them. Buyers generally have a better chance of finding a PML with someone they have a preexisting relationship with, because they trust the buyer to pay them back. I've also seen many of my buyers use PMLs to fund their

down payments and construction costs of the properties they purchase from me. How cool is it that an investor can purchase a fix-and-flip property without using any of their own money, credit, or credentials? This demonstrates the wealth-generating power of real estate investing, and especially of wholesaling.

Cure Period

A cure period is the period in which a buyer or seller may remedy a default on a prespecified aspect of their contract. This could be anything from failing to deposit earnest money to waiving a contingency or to closing escrow. Let's say that a seller is supposed to close escrow on January 14; however, they get food poisoning on the day they're supposed to go to the title company and thus can't make the signing. If the seller does not sign their closing documents on the agreed-upon date, that means the purchase of the property and the deal can't be closed. This essentially puts the seller into default, which allows the buyer to "cure" the seller. I know that sounds scary, but it's not. It means that a grace period is set for the seller to sign the documents before the deal falls through. A cure period can be beneficial to both sellers and buyers because what if we, as the buyer, got food poisoning and couldn't show up to sign our documents on time? This allows for both parties, should something come up, to ensure that all documents and fees are handled by the COE.

Additional Terms

Additional terms refer to anything that needs to be documented in detail that can't be listed in full on the contract itself. We saw an example of this earlier in the additional terms and conditions section that included notes about a tenant living on the property after the close of escrow. The additional terms section can also house the disclosures mentioned in earlier chapters (such as the wholesaler's intent to resell for profit or the seller's notification of defects) and any amendments or clarifications not defined in the standard contract. Here's an example of a standard additional terms section on one of my contracts, with redactions for privacy:

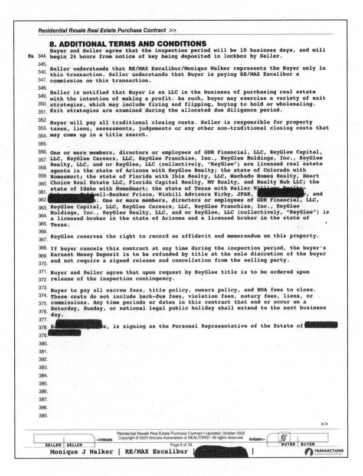

Residential Resale Real Estate Purchase Contract >>

8. ADDITIONAL TERMS AND CONDITIONS

8a. 344. Buyer and Seller agree that the inspection period will be 10 business days, and will begin 24 hours from notice of key being deposited in lockbox by Seller.

345.
346. Seller understands that RE/MAX Excalibur/Monique Walker represents the Buyer only in
347. this transaction. Seller understands that Buyer is paying RE/MAX Excalibur a commission on this transaction.

348.
349. Seller is notified that Buyer is an LLC in the business of purchasing real estate
350. with the intention of making a profit. As such, buyer may exercise a variety of exit strategies, which may include fixing and flipping, buying to hold or wholesaling.
351. Exit strategies are examined during the allocated due diligence period.

352. Buyer will pay all traditional closing costs. Seller is responsible for property
353. taxes, liens, assessments, judgements or any other non-traditional closing costs that
354. may come up in a title search.

355.
356. One or more members, directors or employees of GDR Financial, LLC, KeyGlee Capital,
357. LLC, KeyGlee Careers, LLC, KeyGlee Franchise, Inc., KeyGlee Holdings, Inc., KeyGlee
358. Realty, LLC, and or KeyGlee, LLC (collectively, "KeyGlee") are licensed real estate agents in the state of Arizona with KeyGlee Realty; the state of Colorado with
359. Homesmart; the state of Florida with Ibis Realty, LLC, Machado Homes Realty, Smart
360. Choice Real Estate LLC, Florida Capital Realty, MV Realty, and Realty Hub LLC; the state of Idaho with HomeSmart; the state of Texas with Keller W█████ █████;
361. ████████well-Banker Frisco, Winhill Advisors Kirby, JPAR, ████████r, and
362. ████████k. One or more members, directors or employees of GDR Financial, LLC,
363. KeyGlee Capital, LLC, KeyGlee Careers, LLC, KeyGlee Franchise, Inc., KeyGlee
364. Holdings, Inc., KeyGlee Realty, LLC, and or KeyGlee, LLC (collectively, "KeyGlee") is a licensed broker in the state of Arizona and a licensed broker in the state of
365. Texas.

366.
367. KeyGlee reserves the right to record an affidavit and memorandum on this property.

368. If buyer cancels this contract at any time during the inspection period, the buyer's
369. Earnest Money Deposit is to be refunded by title at the sole discretion of the buyer
370. and not require a signed release and cancellation from the selling party.

371. Buyer and Seller agree that upon request by KeyGlee title is to be ordered upon
372. release of the inspection contingency.

373. Buyer to pay all escrow fees, title policy, owners policy, and HOA fees to close.
374. These costs do not include back-due fees, violation fees, notary fees, liens, or
375. commissions. Any time periods or dates in this contract that end or occur on a
376. Saturday, Sunday, or national legal public holiday shall extend to the next business day.

377.
378. S█████████s, is signing as the Personal Representative of the Estate of █████████
379.
380.
381.
382.
383.
384.
385.
386.
387.
388.
389.

>>

It's fair to say that when in doubt, disclose, disclose, disclose!

What Is an Option Agreement Contract?

An option agreement lets the buyer (or party exercising the option) purchase a property from a seller within a specific timeframe and for a specific price. An example would be a seller saying that a buyer has the option to purchase their property for the next two weeks at $250,000. Why use an option agreement? The main goal is to obtain an equitable interest in a property, as discussed in Chapter 2. This is the interest held by virtue of an equitable title or claimed on equitable grounds. This gives us the right as a wholesaler to buy a property. First, we obtain the equitable interest or gain the legal right to buy a property to then sell that right to a buyer. Option agreements are some of the shortest contract forms that we as wholesalers deal with, but they are some of the more confusing. Nevertheless, these contracts can be incredibly handy because they afford room for flexibility and customization between two parties. Just like with A-B contracts, there are terms you should be familiar with:

- Purchase price.
- Length.
- Nonexclusive.
- Exclusive.
- Consideration.

Purchase Price

In option agreements, the purchase price is the price at which you have the option to purchase a property. Using the above example, if the seller says you can purchase their property for $250,000 in the next two weeks, you have the option to purchase at that price point for only fourteen days. It's an option, not a requirement, so the contractual flexibility is far greater than a purchase and sale agreement. If the seller is asking for more money than your MAO, you'd be better off using an option agreement to gain equitable interest, because it makes the seller aware that you're not a committed purchaser at this price. You may exercise the option should you find another buyer at a price above $250,000, allowing you to make money on the deal.

Length

Length is the amount of the time that you have the option to purchase that property. If the length of time is two weeks, then you have those two weeks to purchase. As with inspection periods, the option period or length is the duration of time where we can exercise the option to purchase (or walk away from) the property.

Nonexclusive

A nonexclusive option agreement is one in which the seller can try to sell the property to someone else within a certain timeframe, even if you've been given the option to purchase at a certain price and within a certain timeframe. Essentially, the seller can shop out the option contract to several buyers at the same time.

Exclusive

As you might expect, an exclusive option agreement is one in which the seller will work only with you to sell their property at a set price and within a set timeframe. Now, exclusive options are what we want as wholesalers. This means even if another buyer or wholesaler is interested in the property, the seller cannot sell that property to them until after your option period has expired.

Consideration

To be legally binding and represent the agreement of transfer of ownership and purchase payment, all contracts are required to include consideration. For our contracts at KeyGlee, we usually put a nominal consideration amount of $10 to help establish that a value is being exchanged between parties.

Option Agreement Summary

When would you ever use an option agreement? Option agreements are used when a seller wants a much higher price than your MAO calculation. Again, there's nothing wrong with that; a homeowner is attached to their home, regardless of its condition, and depending on the situation, they may need as much cash as they can get. In such cases, option agreements give wholesalers the opportunity to take that seller's price point and use the time period to see if you can find a buyer interested in the property for a higher price (because the new prices include your fee). Sometimes it works, sometimes it doesn't. With an exclusive agreement, the seller is letting you see if you can market the contract for their property at the price point they're looking for in its current condition. With a nonexclusive option, the seller is putting out an all-points bulletin and will go with the first wholesaler or buyer who can give them the price they want. Again, this might work depending on the property, the situation, and the condition—especially with exclusive agreements—by allowing you to help the seller as best you can. If a price doesn't work for you, that doesn't mean that it won't work for another wholesaler or another buyer.

This is why I recommend to many wholesalers that they use non-exclusive option agreements, especially if they're just starting out in wholesaling. When it comes to these agreements, the key to making it work is communication. One of the biggest downsides to using nonexclusive option agreements is when a seller finds a buyer and doesn't tell you. It is beyond frustrating to find a buyer only to find out the property is no longer available.

What Are Assignment Contracts?

An assignment contract is the transfer of a contract from one party to another. For example, you as the wholesaler (Person B in an A-B contract) contracted to buy a property from a homeowner (Person A), but you then want to sell the contract to another buyer (Person C). Assignments are extremely common in wholesaling because they're what acquisitions wholesalers use to transfer the contract made with the seller to the buyer that you found. Assignment contracts are most often used for:

- Wholesale transactions.
- Acquisition co-wholesale transactions.
- Disposition co-wholesale transactions.

Assignment contracts are used when you have an established contract with the seller in place and you are assigning your role as the buyer to another person. Let's look at an example:

ASSIGNMENT SALE

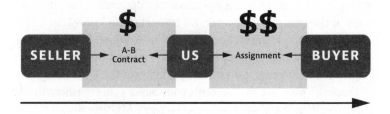

In this image, the Seller (Person A) has signed an A-B contract (also called a Purchase and Sale Agreement) with Us (Person B). As the acquisitions wholesaler, we want to assign this contract to our Buyer through an assignment contract. The Buyer takes over the position of Person B (formerly Us) in the A-B contract. The Buyer pays us an assignment fee (think of it as a finder's fee) for taking over our position in the A-B contract. Let's check out some terminology when using assignment contracts:

- COE.
- EMD.
- Title company.
- Assignor.
- Assignee.
- Sale price.
- Address.
- Assessor's parcel number (APN).

COE

The close of escrow is the same as discussed above. The COE on the assignment contract must match the time duration on the A-B Standard contract.

EMD

Again, the EMD is a good faith amount due from the buyer. The EMD, unlike the COE, does not need to match the amount in the A-B contract. In the A-B contract between you and the seller, your earnest money is based on an amount agreed upon by you and the seller. The amount is subjective and can be as little as $10, although in most cases, this amount is equal to about 1 percent of the purchase price of the contract. However, it's important to know that EMD amounts vary by market. For example, in Arizona, I typically put up $2,000 for EMD regardless of sales price and have rarely been challenged to increase it. In the assignment contract, the EMD acts as a security measure that cements your buyer's commitment to the purchase. Wholesalers typically elect larger EMD amounts for their assignments to ensure that a buyer will close the transaction. The larger the EMD, the less likely your buyer will walk away from the purchase. It's common to see wholesalers require nonrefundable EMD amounts ranging from $5,000 to $25,000.

Title Company

The title company on the assignment contract must be the same company as listed on the A-B contract. This is because both of these contracts will be delivered and managed by that same title company.

Assignor

The assignor is the person who is assigning the contract. In this example, it is Us.

Assignee

The assignee is the person who is being assigned the contract. In this example, it is the Buyer. Ask the assignee how they would like to be named in the B-C contract (vesting, aka the buyer's entity name).

Sale Price

The sale price is the original purchase price plus the assignment fee. For example, the A-B contract states that you'll purchase a property from the Seller for $245,000. In the assignment contract, you'll include the $245,000 plus your assignment fee of $20,000, so the Buyer will have a contract with you that shows a sale price of $265,000. The EMD is based on this new price.

Address
This is pretty easy. It's the address of the property.

APN
The assessor's parcel number is a unique number that's assigned by the local assessor's office to every real estate transaction in the area. It's used to keep track of information that's related to our subject property.

A purchase and sale agreement is between you and the seller, and assignment contracts are between you and the buyer who will ultimately buy the property. Now let's look at the details of these contracts.

What Is a B-C Contract?

Once you secure to the rights to your property as the buyer in an A-B contract, you now need to create a new contract if you decide to sell it. B-C contracts are most prominently used when selling your contract on a wholesale property to another investor or buyer. B-C contracts are written to protect the seller during the process of a property sale and redefine terms for a new escrow agreement with the new buyer. However, there are some other ways to use B-C contracts, such as:

- Selling a wholesale property from one entity to another entity that you own.
- Selling a wholesale property directly to the end buyer.
- Selling an off-market property that you personally own to an investor or buyer.

Some of the terminology when using B-C contracts will look familiar:

COE
As before with the assignment contract, the close of escrow date needs to match on the B-C contract and across all contracts.

EMD Amount
The amount of earnest money that the end buyer is going to put down should be on the B-C contract. This number is going to be different from the amount of EMD that you are putting down with the seller on the A-B contract.

Title Company
As before, the title company on the B-C contract must match the company on both the assignment contract and the A-B contract.

Seller
The seller in this case is actually the buyer on the A-B contract, which is *you*. Because you are assigning this contract to another buyer, you have now become the *seller* in this transaction.

Assignee
Just like we are now the seller in this contract, the end buyer is now the vesting entity.

There's one more contract agreement we need to look at, but I first want to take a moment and discuss important clauses that come up in each of these.

Important Contract Clauses
Contract clauses are provisions or conditions that specify the rights, duties, or obligations of all parties. Clauses cover a wide range of topics, such as payment terms, resolutions of disputes, any types of terminations, etc. Each contract will have its own specific clauses.

The following are some I use with my own deals.

A-B CONTRACT CLAUSES

There are two clauses that I tend to use in my A-B contracts: agency disclosure, and intent for financial gain. If you remember from Chapter 3, there has been a big push in several states for wholesalers to get real estate licenses and/or be placed under the authority of the NAR for a more regulated industry.

In many real estate transactions, agents must provide if they are licensed in the state where they practice. Again, no agent can practice real estate without having a license. An agency disclosure clause states that you *or a member of your business* is a licensed agent within a particular city or state. If you are not licensed to practice in a certain state, someone who is licensed in that state (an agent or agency) can assist you, as long as all parties follow state laws and regulations.

The other clause that I use is the intent for financial gain. This clause tells the title company, the seller, the real estate attorney, and everyone else that I, as the acquisitions wholesaler, am purchasing this property for investment and that my intent is to make a profit on the resale of that property.

ASSIGNMENT CONTRACT CLAUSES

One major reason to use clauses in all real estate contracts is the earnest money deposit. In the assignment contract, it is a good faith payment from the buyer that shows their commitment to the purchase of the property from you. In assignment contracts, the EMD is always specified in the form of a cashier's check or a wire payment. The reason for this is because the title company can take five or more days to cash a personal check. If your inspection period is for that same timeframe, you want to make sure that you've received that earnest money in the fastest way possible.

Most EMDs are due to the title company by 10:00 a.m. the next business day after a contract is signed. This clause can be changed, depending on the situation and the time of purchase. For example, if a contract's closing date falls on a federal holiday, then the next business day would be the day after the observed holiday.

You can also change the time of close. For example, the end of day on a Friday or Saturday helps buyers with a little more time, but you want to ensure that you and they get through the process in a timely manner. One reason to add a due date in an assignment contract is because it gives you the ability and right to cancel the assignment contract due to nonperformance. This means that if you've given a due date in the contract and the buyer misses that deadline, you can cancel the contract with them if they are outside of their cure period. Without this clause, you are prevented from canceling that assignment contract and finding another buyer. Without a buyer, you'd need to cancel your A-B contract with the seller. These are the cancellations we want to avoid and that give wholesaling a bad name.

An EMD is immediately nonrefundable if the buyer does not close on the agreed-upon date and time, which helps to keep people honest. As an acquisitions wholesaler, when you put out word of a property that you want to assign, you'll get a lot of interested people. Having a nonrefundable EMD means that you avoid a situation where one buyer agrees to buy the property but then backs out right before COE. If that buyer has signed the assignment contract and has put down a nonrefundable EMD, it boosts their commitment to buy the property.

Finally, as the assignor, you retain control over the EMD that you put down in the A-B contract. This is important because if you must cancel an assignment contract and also the A-B agreement, it would be easy for the title company to refund your EMD to the canceled buyer, who has taken our place in the A-B contract. Obviously, that's not good, so this clause ensures that if an assignment contract is canceled, and a purchase and sale agreement is canceled, your EMD is returned to you.

You want clauses in assignment contracts that revert all of your rights as the assignor back to you. For example, if a buyer fails to close by COE, your rights revert back to you and you can create a new assignment contract with another buyer.

Here's a sample of an assignment contract that we use at KeyGlee:

Assignment of Residential Purchase Contract

For the Assignment Fee set forth below, and other good and valuable consideration, and the mutual benefits to be delivered by all parties to this agreement, the undersigned KeyGlee Investments, LLC (Assignor) does hereby assign unto ▓▓▓▓▓▓▓▓▓▓▓▓▓▓ (Assignee) all rights, interest, suits, claims, and title to a contract of sale concerning such property known as 7028 S 55th Ave, Phoenix, AZ 85041 with an APN of ▓▓▓▓▓ (the "Subject Property"). Original property escrow is held at West Title Agency of Arizona▓▓▓▓▓▓▓▓).

Provided, however, no warranties of any kind whatsoever are made incident to this Assignment and the Assignee accepts all rights, obligations, and responsibilities of the Purchase Contract concerning the Subject Property and agrees to close on or before the date set forth therein. If escrow fails to close on or before **12pm MST August 15th, 2019**, all rights to the Purchase Contract immediately transfer back to Assignor.

Assignee herein agrees to deposit Assignment Earnest Money of **$3,000.00** By 10AM AZ time on the day following execution of this Assignment in the form of cashier's check or wired funds into escrow.

Disbursement of Fees, Purchase Contract Earnest Money and Assignment Earnest Money shall be as follows: The Assignment Fee will be calculated as the difference between the Sales Price of the Contract, which is the subject of the Assignment, and the amount of **$194,900.00**. The Assignment Fee will be disbursed to Assignor at the close of escrow and paid through escrow.

The Assignment Earnest Money is to be credited towards the Assignee's purchase costs at the close of escrow. Assignee will forfeit all Assignment Earnest Money to Assignor if escrow does not close due to Assignee's cancellation or failure to perform under the Purchase Contract or this Assignment for any reason other than seller's inability to provide clear title by the closing date or breach of the Purchase Contract by seller.

In the event of a dispute between Assignor and Assignee regarding the Assignment Earnest Money deposited with West Title Agency of Arizona, Assignor and Assignee authorize West Title Agency of Arizona to release the Assignment Earnest Money pursuant to the terms and conditions of this Assignment in its sole and absolute discretion. Assignor and Assignee agree to hold harmless and indemnify West Title Agency of Arizona against any claim, action, or lawsuit of any kind, and from any loss, judgment, or expense, including costs and attorney fees, arising from or relating in any way to the release of the Assignment Earnest Money as provided herein. The Earnest

B-C CONTRACT CLAUSES

The B-C contract is the second contract signed between you as the wholesaler and the buyer. This contract replaces your name on the A-B contract with the buyer's name, making them the ultimate buyer of the property. What this does is remove your name since you are no longer acting as the buyer in the situation and are now the seller of the contract.

B-C contract clauses are similar to assignment contract clauses. For instance, the EMD must be made by either a cashier's check or wire payment transfer, and it's usually due by 10:00 a.m. the next business day after a B-C contract is signed. The EMD is immediately nonrefundable to the buyer. One clause with a key difference is that when canceling an assignment contract, the EMD goes back to the assignor and all rights also revert back to the wholesaler. In B-C contracts, there is a clause that if the buyer doesn't close by COE by the specified time (12:00 p.m. on my contracts), then the buyer's EMD goes to the seller (Person A). This pushes buyers to complete the purchase process. However, if the buyer cannot meet the deadline, it gives us as the assignors the time to find another buyer while still making the end-of-day deadline to deliver EMD to the title company (now paid for by us since the buyer has walked away). We can continue to shop for a buyer, which helps out the seller. Below are sample clauses that KeyGlee uses in our B-C contracts:

**REAL ESTATE
SALE AND PURCHASE CONTRACT**

For good and valuable consideration mutually acknowledged exchanged between the parties, this Contract is made by and between:

Seller: KeyGlee, LLC

and

Buyer

for the purchase and sale of certain real property ("Transaction") commonly known as: **211 E McDonald St, Phoenix, AZ 85023 with an APN of** ("Property").

    1. Effective Date. As used herein, the "Effective Date" for this Contract is the 24th day of April, 2019.

    2. Purchase Price; Payment. The total purchase price for the Property is which amount, including the Deposit, shall be paid in cash upon Closing.

    3. Non-Refundable Deposit. Except for Seller's obligation to comply with the terms of Section 12 of this Contract, this Transaction is not subject to any other conditions of whatsoever kind, including without limitation, Buyer's ability to secure financing and any property inspections undertaken subsequent to the Effective Date. Simultaneous with its execution of this Contract, Buyer is tendering to Seller an earnest money deposit of $5,000 that is non-refundable immediately ("Deposit "). However, Buyer warrants that before signing this Contract and tendering the Deposit, Buyer carefully and thoroughly reviewed the terms of this Contract, including without limitation, Sections 10 and 11 below. Accordingly, Seller shall only be obligated to refund the Deposit to Buyer if Seller is unable to produce clear title.

Joint Venture Contracts

Joint ventures can help you get your feet wet as a new wholesaler and build lasting relationships with other wholesalers, fix-and-flippers, and real estate investors. As I mentioned earlier in the book, it's a strategy that I encourage often. What is a JV, and why would you want to split your potential earning on a deal?

WHAT IS A JOINT VENTURE?

A joint venture is a business arrangement where two or more individuals agree to work together on a specific project or business venture. Everyone involved will typically contribute resources and share in the profits of that venture. JVs have many forms and structures related to what each individual wants to achieve. JVs allow us to pursue opportunities that would be difficult to do on our own.

You may have heard of popular JVs among famous businesses. For example, in 2007, the Walt Disney Company, News Corporation, Comcast NBCUniversal, and Providence Equity Partners were looking for ways to run programming from several titans within the entertainment industry. At the time, Netflix, through its DVD subscription site, had begun to offer subscribers the option to stream some of their movies and TV shows directly into homes without the mailing back and forth of DVDs. The idea was appealing and offered a new perspective on what the internet could do and where entertainment appeared to be headed. What is this JV, you ask?

It's a little streaming site called Hulu. All of the aforementioned companies came together to invest in Hulu, purposely creating a competitor for Netflix in the online streaming entertainment space. Hulu is just one example of companies joining their resources and knowledge to build something new, and to share in its profits.

Another example is the Curiosity rover, which landed on Mars in 2012. It was the result of United Launch Alliance, a joint venture between industry-leading aerospace companies Boeing and Lockheed Martin.

A joint venture between General Electric and Microsoft created Caradigm, a company that uses data to improve health care quality and patient experience, and created Predix Platform, an application development platform that equips businesses to build and deploy Internet of Things applications.

HOW JOINT VENTURES WORK IN REAL ESTATE

For real estate investors and wholesalers, JVs allow us to explore deals that we might not have access to or even know about, and allow us to make new connections and create relationships. Your weakness is your JV partner's strength, and vice versa. Maybe you're an introvert and you struggle to find the right buyers, or maybe you struggle with the math to comp deals. With a JV, you're partnering with someone who complements your skill set. It's an incredible tool to get your deals to closing.

JV agreements protect everyone in the deal by ensuring that everyone gets paid by the title company. The title company is the one who not only collects all of the documentation but also disperses the money to each person involved in the transaction. This legitimizes you as one principal in the original contract.

Creating a JV means you have a *temporary* partnership with another person or a group of people. A *permanent* partnership means that you own an LLC together, share a company bank account, and so on. Having a JV is more like dating: You agree to work on a particular deal or two. A permanent partnership is more like marriage: You share a business entity, banking accounts, revenue, expenses, and so on. Rahima, Josiah, Hunter, and I did hundreds of JV deals together for about a year before we formed KeyGlee (and we're still going strong after six wonderful years). A JV is a useful dating mechanism that offers you the opportunity to work with someone without moving into a full-scale partnership too quickly, if you do at all. For example, in a joint venture, you might use the option agreement. As discussed earlier in the chapter, an option agreement gives the seller (the JV) the ability to sell a property for a specific amount of time and price. Having that agreement gives everyone in the JV an equitable interest to sell that option to someone else, and if you have a nonexclusive contract with the original seller, there are now several people trying to bring in a buyer.

HOW TO DETERMINE IF A JV IS WORTHWHILE

Creating JVs has become quite popular, with real estate investors now realizing that collaboration is far better than competition, so more are open to the idea of creating joint ventures. As with real-life dating, there will be instances that may feel uncomfortable. This is common if you don't know a potential JV partner well, or in some cases you don't know the person at all. In these cases, it's important to ask qualifying questions to better understand each other.

What questions should you ask? Well, that depends on two things: whether you're trying to bring a buyer into the deal or you already have a property under contract.

Bringing the Buyer
If I'm bringing a buyer to the table—that is, I have a potential buyer who is interested in a particular property—I want to know if my potential JV partner already has the contract. The questions to ask include:
- What is the address of the property?
- What does the property look like?
- Who is the title company?
- When is the close of escrow (COE)?

These should be easy questions to answer for an acquisitions wholesaler who has signed the A-B contract and is looking for a buyer. If those questions can't be answered quickly and easily, then you know the person doesn't have the signed contract yet.

Now, let's say I'm the acquisition wholesaler, and I want to vet a possible JV partner who has a buyer for this property. Then I would ask:
- Have you worked with this buyer before?
- Do you have other deals in this area?
- Do you have other property addresses that you've flipped before?
- Is there any proof of funds that you're willing to provide?
- How quickly can your buyer close?
- Is your buyer using cash or hard money?

A disposition wholesaler might not have all these answers, but they can ask their buyer. Not only are you vetting a JV partner, but you're also making sure that they vet the buyer. This helps you to evaluate and judge the seriousness of the potential buyer.

Below is a sample joint venture agreement:

JOINT VENTURE AGREEMENT

This joint venture agreement made and entered into this **19th** day of **June, 2020** (the "Execution date")

BETWEEN

_____

_____

(Individually the "Member" and collectively the "Members").

BACKGROUND
A. The Members wish to enter an association of mutual benefit and agree to jointly invest and set up a joint venture enterprise.
B. This agreement sets out the terms and conditions governing this association.

IN CONSIDERATION OF and as a condition of the Members entering into this agreement and other valuable consideration, the receipt and sufficiency of which consideration is acknowledged, the Members agree as follows:

FORMATION
1. By this agreement the Members enter into a joint venture (the "Venture") in accordance with the laws of the state of Idaho. The rights and obligations of the Members will be as stated in the applicable legislation of the state of Idaho (the "Act") except as otherwise provided here.

Name
2. The business name of the Venture will be

_____

Purpose
3. The exclusive purpose of the Venture (the "Purpose") will be

_____

Joint ventures can be fantastic, but they can also be a tough sell. People have to figure out how they're supposed to work together and who should be doing what, when, why, and how. What can really help with this is making sure that everyone involved is able to divide the work with each other, be accountable for their assigned duties, and work in a collaborative fashion with each other. However, there are ways to set expectations and methods to divide the work.

Create Social Networks of Accountability

In general, you need to create a network of people that will hold you—and you, them—accountable for the tasks that everyone says they will complete. Accountability groups aren't to nag; the purpose is to support and motivate everyone to stay on track with their self-assigned goals. This means regular check-ins or meetings to update each other on work and to share encouragement. That encouragement builds trust, community, and friendship, and eventually those bonds begin to deepen. With a foundation built on trust, the greater the possibility to do deals together and the stronger your networks will be. You can find accountability groups on social media, at in-person meetings, and by asking people you trust.

Collaboration over Competition

I've mentioned collaboration over competition several times throughout the book, and now's the time to explain what I mean in detail.

In many industries, there is a mindset that says if you want to be the best and get to the top of the ladder, you have to push people out of the way to get there. Real estate is one of those industries because everyone is fighting to get that next deal, sell that next house, and get the next commission. This is one reason that wholesalers got a bad rap: Many prioritized competition over collaboration to make a quick buck, and it didn't matter who got hurt in the process. It's the idea that a lone wolf is far more successful than being a part of a pack. I think that's the wrong attitude. When you collaborate with others, you achieve more than you would independently or by working against each other. Your success isn't just about how many deals you do. Your reputation is based on how well you work with others and is directly tied to your potential for future collaborations—in other words, it directly affects how many deals others will bring to you. If you're too hard to work with or prioritize competition over collaboration, you will miss out on relationships and JV deals, losing millions of dollars in sales because of your poor reputation. If this sounds like you, now is a perfect opportunity to work on your mindset. We talked about this in Chapter 4. If you can recognize when you're exhibiting competitive behaviors, you can learn how release your ego to make the changes needed to be on the right path in real estate.

Honoring collaboration over competition means:
- Being supportive of others and their deals.
- Working together to find or close deals.
- Providing value to buyers, sellers, and other wholesalers.

Being competitive means:
- Holding a grudge when someone else gets a deal you wanted.
- Being jealous of other wholesalers' successes.
- Withholding resources, tools, or information that could help buyers, sellers, or other wholesalers.

Here's the takeaway: You gain so much more by collaborating rather than competing with others. In earlier chapters, I talked about Brent Daniels and Pace Morby. These guys are my "competition" when it comes to getting deals done. However, we routinely speak at each other's events to educate the community. I have invited them both to be a part of my mastermind group, and every Monday we do our podcast *Wholesale Hotline* together.

Pace and I were on a speaking tour arranged by someone else when we discussed how we started in the business and how we met each other. That was the first time we actively talked about creating our own speaking tour, despite being competitors. Now, could we have done separate speaking tours, with me talking about my work and Pace talking about his? Absolutely, but it wouldn't have been as good for our audiences or for us.

You might be thinking, "Jamil, if these guys are your real estate competitors, why are you collaborating with them on other things?" I do because they are two of the most intelligent and sweetest guys I've ever met. Just because we compete on some deals doesn't mean that we can't or won't work together in other ways related to real estate. We all have skills and approaches that are different from each other. I could easily work just with my own business lines, find deals, and talk to sellers all day long—and there's nothing wrong with that. You might think it would be easier to start your wholesale journey by setting up your business and working alone.

But having people you respect and like in your network means having people hold you accountable while providing you support and guidance. The meaning of this can't be measured. Well, technically, it can, and academics have been studying this for decades to learn how relationships affect people psychologically. Encouraging others, and them encouraging you, increases levels of confidence and feelings of accomplishment. Don't you feel good when someone tells you that you've done a great job or when getting a "Thanks so much!" after you've helped someone? I could've done my own deals without my sister Rahima's help. Josiah, Hunter, and I could have certainly continued working together without forming KeyGlee—but we never would've achieved the level of success we have if we'd worked alone.

It was this successful collaborative business that caught the eye of A&E and led us to getting our own TV show. Never in a million years did we believe that we would be on TV, but that's what happened. Highly qualified experts learn to collaborate, not compete, and others will notice.

I mentioned that my AstroFlipping community members will squad up with Pace's SubTo members. Hundreds of deals have happened because of these collaborations. Pace and I actively encourage our members to partner together, and to assist and guide one another. Both of our communities have seasoned industry wholesalers who offer support to those just starting out. Many former newbies are experienced wholesalers who now mentor new investors starting on their journey. In writing this book, I've tried to mentor you, and hopefully you've gained enough knowledge to move forward with your wholesaling future. Who knows? Maybe one day we'll collaborate on a deal together.

WHOLESALE SUCCESS STORY
Relationships = Revenue with Jacob Simpson

It took me a lot longer than it should have to get my first wholesale deal. Most people get theirs within three to six months. But me? A year and a half. Now, there were a couple of reasons for that, but the main reason it took so long was the lack of relationships I was creating.

I got started with the direct-to-seller model, where you reach out to homeowners directly and ask if they want to sell their house. I made tens of thousands of calls, sent a bunch of mail, texted tons of numbers, and even tried door knocking, but nothing was working. And to make it worse, every promising lead that came in seemed to get locked up by another wholesaler. Distraught from months of no results, I decided to reach out to the other wholesaler and ask if they'd be open to partnering with me rather than competing. To my surprise, they were!

This is where things started to turn for me. Whenever I had a new lead, my wholesale partner would help me comp it, put together a buy number, lock it up, sell the deal, and sometimes even talk to the seller for me. My mind was blown! I was wasting months of my time trying to do this myself when I could have just worked with someone else. And it was a win-win for both of us: They got a lead they didn't have prior, I got help and was able to learn the business, and we both got paid if it closed. That's the power of a relationship!

Although I was closing deals after partnering up, it was still a slow start. I was doing about one deal every four months. Out of curiosity, I asked the other wholesaler where most of their deals came from. Their answer? Through other wholesalers like me. This really got me thinking, because most "gurus" weren't talking about this. Ironically, as I was trying to figure out how to work with others, an ad by Jamil popped up and interrupted my social media scrolling. I'll never forget it. Jamil is in an igloo, ice all over him. Shivering, he says, "Are you tired of COLD calls?" It's like he was talking directly to me. So, I reached out and joined Jamil's community.

Now before learning from Jamil, I had only done three deals in about two years. I was getting deterred, but I was determined to make this work. I took what Jamil was teaching and changed my entire business model. No joke. I canceled all my direct-to-seller marketing and started working directly with wholesalers. It was a major shift after two years of direct-to-seller, but it was the best thing I've ever done. It gave me a new perspective on wholesaling. Instead of a transactional business (doing one deal with a homeowner), I was now looking at this as a relationship business (doing multiple deals with one wholesaler)—a business model that was much better suited to my style, personality, and goals.

Since then, my business has 10Xed! All I do is work with wholesalers and real estate agents, many of whom are my close friends now. I've closed over sixty transactions and helped wholesalers make over $1.5 million in assignment fees...all because of relationships. Relationships are literally the backbone of my business. They're the reason I've grown to this level, and they'll be the reason I continue to grow. As the saying goes, "Relationships over Revenue." That's pretty much the basis of my business. The revenue will come with the relationships you make. No one is self-made!

A QUICK RECAP

- There are five types of contracts:
  - **A-B contracts:** Between a seller (Person A) and buyer (Person B); it opens up the first escrow on a property.
  - **Option agreement contracts:** Allows a buyer or party to exercise the option to purchase a property from a seller within a specified timeframe and for a specific price.
  - **Assignment contracts:** Assigns the position of ownership from you to a buyer.
  - **B-C contracts:** Removes your name as Person B on the A-B contract and inserts Person C's name.
  - **Joint venture (JV) contracts:** Temporary partnerships between two or more entities working together to close a deal.

- Contract clauses are provisions or conditions that specify the rights, duties, and obligations of the signatories. This includes disclosures such as the intent to profit from the sale of a property.
- Collaboration over competition is vital. You can partner with one or more people who complement your skills and you complement theirs; it helps you create a network; it builds your reputation; and it allows you to participate in deals you might never have found otherwise.

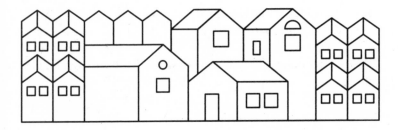

CHAPTER 10
How to Scale Your Wholesaling Empire

Throughout this book, you've learned the basics of wholesale real estate: what it is, its background within the industry, and the legalities and regulations surrounding it. You've examined where your mind and perspectives are and how they play into your business and personal decisions. You know the different aspects that make up wholesaling—from what it means to be an acquisitions wholesaler or a dispositions wholesaler to understanding value to finding and calculating your numbers correctly to secure a contract. You also now know the different types of contracts and the situations in which to use them.

Now, we're going to pull all of these aspects together to not just build up a wholesale real estate business but also scale it to a revolving door of profit.

Here are the six steps to scaling your wholesale empire that we'll cover in this chapter:

- Step 1: Establish Your Mission and Vision
- Step 2: Establish Your Culture and Core Values
- Step 3: How to Hire the Right People
- Step 4: Establish an Organizational Structure
- Step 5: Determine How to Measure Success
- Step 6: Scale Your Business

First, we'll take a look at how we scaled KeyGlee from an idea into an empire.

The Growth of KeyGlee

In Chapter 7, we talked about how KeyGlee saw the opportunity to bridge a gap between acquisitions and dispositions wholesalers in the industry, helping close more deals and foster relationships. Because KeyGlee was able to provide that solution, we became a national powerhouse with franchises spreading across the country. In this chapter, we'll walk you through the exact path we followed to scale this industry-leading company—because it wasn't all smooth sailing. It took some honest reflection on our goals, understanding our strengths and weaknesses, and learning how a business changes as it grows from five people to ten, fifty, and eventually more than one hundred people. What we'll share below is everything we learned and everything we wish we'd known from the moment we got started back in 2016.

When you're first building your business, these are the most fundamental questions you need to ask yourself:

- What is the end goal of my company?
- What are my professional strengths and weaknesses?

I implore you to investigate both of these questions honestly, because they might not be as easily answered as you think. If we hadn't addressed them before we launched KeyGlee, things might have been very different.

We didn't realize it at the time, but one of the key elements of our success was having the right four founders from the start. The combination of skills and personalities was what our company needed, and it provided an incredible foundation for growth. As I mentioned in Chapter 4, I had a massive mindset shift right before I met and joined the KeyGlee team. I went from undergoing a miserable spiral that almost cost me my family to using meditation to focus my passion for real estate and take back the reins in my career. All of this resulted in the idea for KeyGlee—but before I could put this idea into motion, I had to convince other people that it was strong enough to build a business on. I wanted to create a legal and ethical solution to a problem I saw in the industry and become a reliable disposition resource for wholesalers to reduce the amount of failed deals. I had shopped this idea around Phoenix to no avail, until finally I met Josiah and Hunter, two of the future founders of KeyGlee. They had been investing in real estate in their spare time, specializing in dispositions, while my sister Rahima and I were regularly crushing our own acquisitions deals. It seemed like the perfect fit. Rahima had been a licensed real estate agent for many years before this, so she was well aware of the market in the late 2010s; honestly, she was the first agent I worked with as we began doing deals together.

Luckily, the stars aligned to ensure that Rahima would help me get back on the real estate path, that I would have the idea for KeyGlee, that Hunter and Josiah would join us, and that together we would create one of the fastest-growing wholesale real estate franchises in the nation. Call it fate, call it faith, call it Craigslist (not really), but we ended up finding each other.

Once we formed our team and were all-in on the idea for KeyGlee, we knew that certain operational processes were necessary for the business to succeed long term. We needed to have strong organization, consistent cash flow, tons of new leads coming through the door, and the right technology to bring our idea to life. Trust me, it takes a lot to go from a great idea to a functioning business.

First of all, we needed capital—all of it came from Rahima and me, as did the leads for every deal we closed in our first year of business. We were happy to contribute to getting KeyGlee off the ground.

From the beginning, I provided the initial idea, the initial funding, the initial deals; and I was happy to do it. So it might surprise you to learn that I wasn't and never have been KeyGlee's CEO … nor did I want to be.

I knew that while I could (and did) contribute a lot to this business, I was not the best person for the job. Josiah was. And I was happy to help get him there. In Josiah, I saw values, skill sets, and the vision that a great CEO needed. He lights up every room he walks into, bringing a sincerity and strategic nature that blends perfectly into the leader we all want at our helm. He also had skills in cutting-edge technology that went almost entirely over my head. I'm a paper and pen kind of guy; tech is not my cup of tea. But we needed someone with the tech and organizational skills to make this company a successful twenty-first-century business, and Josiah had them in spades.

I brought hustle, grit, knowledge, relationship skills, a network of suppliers, agent deal flow, and a $1 million check to start the business up. However, I didn't let my contributions or my ego stop me from looking objectively at what or who the business *needed* at the top. I was able to take a step back and realized that of the four of us, I wasn't the best person for this role. If I hadn't spent years learning how to overcome my own ego, I may not have made the same decision. I was truthful with myself and knew where my and my other team members' strengths and weaknesses were. We were able to take an objective look at ourselves as fully rounded human beings and recognize where in the organization we fit best. Looking at our shortcomings didn't make us weaker. In fact, addressing them and allowing our team to focus on our strengths made us infinitely stronger.

It's important as you build and scale your business that you encourage this kind of self-awareness, share responsibilities, give credit to others, and allow people to be in positions that will help move your business forward—even if it means they will be in a position that's higher than yours in the company. Real leaders will still be leaders regardless of their title. Our self-awareness, clear roles, and understanding of each other's strengths and weaknesses were crucial at this beginning stage. It helped build a strong foundation within our core leadership team that would carry us forward as we began to expand our workforce, outline our vision, and grow as a company.

As we go through the six steps I mentioned at the start of this chapter, you'll get an understanding of how we approached each of these steps at KeyGlee, and how you can build your business in a similar way.

Step 1: Establish Your Mission and Vision

Before you start putting your wholesale business together, you should establish the mission and vision for your company. Truthfully, this will evolve and change over time. Your mission and vision won't always be 100 percent perfect right from the start. However, taking the time to talk through this with your team and align on what you want the company to achieve and look like as it grows will set you up for a strong start.

A lot of people tend to confuse mission and vision, but they aren't the same. Your business's *mission statement* defines your company's purpose: How will it change the world, and how will it impact the niche of your choice? The best mission statements are short, sweet, and unifying. It should be something your company can rally around as you grow. Most entrepreneurs start out with the mission to make a lot of money. While that's understandable, it's not a strong unifying purpose because it lacks any mention of impact or desire to improve their chosen niche. Instead, you should think about three main focuses:

1. Identify the niche you want to participate in.
2. Identify what the pain points/challenges are within that niche, and how your company will combat or resolve them.
3. Write your mission statement.

Our current mission statement at KeyGlee is to "Bless millions through investment by changing the barrier of real estate." But it wasn't always that short and sweet. When we started, we didn't truly know what our company was going to do. We only knew that we wanted to create a God-fearing company that did well; a great company that did good. Ultimately, as we grew, we narrowed our focus down to impacting wholesale real estate across the world, while also impacting the lives of our employees. Simplifying and refining this as you grow is very common and allows you to refocus your mission as your company grows and changes.

Your business's *vision* is the description of what your business will look like when you're achieving your mission. It's the actual blueprint of what achieving success looks like in a specific timeframe. For example, in five years' time, how many employees will you have? How many markets will your company operate in? How many units are you closing in a month? How about in a year? What size and type of office will you work out of? All of these details come together to form a practical vision of what the future of your company will look like.

Simply saying "We'll be the biggest company in the Phoenix market" isn't enough. You're leaving too much open for interpretation, and your team may not all be on the same page for what "the biggest" or "the best" means for them. The more detailed you can be, the easier it will be for everyone at your company to visualize what the future will look like, and the better they can work together to achieve that future. There's serious power in having everybody on your team working toward the same goal—give them one worthy of their hard work.

Step 2: Establish Your Culture and Core Values

COMPANY CULTURE

Once you have your mission and vision identified, the next step is establishing your company culture and core values. Like your mission and vision, this is something that will emerge and evolve over time as your team grows. The purpose of company culture is to help align your business and employees toward the outcomes that matter. It also means defining what you *don't* want your culture to look like.

Being culturally aligned or being a culture fit within a business gets thrown around a lot these days. What does it mean? How does a company create a culture, and how does someone become a cultural fit in a company? To be culturally aligned, a business needs to implement policies and practices that foster inclusivity, respect, and open-mindedness to create an environment that promotes collaboration and understanding among employees with different cultural backgrounds. That's a very simplified explanation, and many businesses have their own company culture.

For example, Google is known for having a company culture that encourages creativity and innovation and is built on transparency, open communication, and collaboration. That makes sense, considering Google is the company behind some of the biggest programs worldwide, and despite some of the incidents that might be happening at their home campus, that ideal is still promoted. Google provides on-site wellness centers, choices of healthy food for meals, and generous time-off policies.

As stated in our mission statement, KeyGlee has a culture that is based on faith, integrity, and love for one another. We believe in a foundation of love, where we strive to be positive, ensure that we are generally helping others and our community, and believe in collaboration over competition. The four of us saw how other businesses and even other wholesalers get taken down from the challenges of gossip, backstabbing, and other woes because of misunderstandings and miscommunications. We wanted our company to be an environment where all our employees, franchisees, and team members could succeed in everything they do—not just the work they do for us.

Here are four core tenets of culture that I'd recommend every company start with:

1. **Foundation of Love/Assumption of Positive Intent**
   - We encourage people to assume positive intent in situations where somebody's actions or intentions are open to interpretation.
   - *Example:* You say hello to a coworker and they don't acknowledge you or look up from their desk. You may think they have a problem with you or were ignoring you, but they actually have headphones in and didn't even hear you. Assuming positive intent allows you not to take that personally.

2. Avoid Gossip

- The long and short of it is don't say something negative about someone who isn't present, and don't speak on behalf of a situation you're not involved in.
- *Example:* You unintentionally overhear somebody talking negatively about a coworker, and you go tell the coworker in question what the others were saying. Instead, you should go directly to the coworkers speaking negatively and tell them if they have a problem to resolve that directly—or remove yourself from the situation entirely.

3. Take Responsibility

- We encourage radical ownership of our mistakes and avoid placing blame on others. As soon as you blame something else, you're no longer in control of the situation.
- *Example:* A manager's results are slipping, and rather than owning that outcome as the leader, they blame various members of their team or other departments for the failure. A good leader will take ownership and work toward a better outcome with their team rather than shifting blame.

4. Break the Cycle of Shame

- Many of us will allow external factors such as positive or negative feedback to impact our emotional well-being. Whether it's negative feedback making us feel shameful or it's positive feedback making us complacent, we always encourage people to focus on improving the work itself rather than just the feedback they're getting.
- *Example:* You come into the office excited for the day, but in your 1:1 with your manager, they give you some tough feedback about the quality of your work. You then allow this to get in your head, putting you in a bad mood and leaving you unproductive for the rest of the day. Do your best not to let this push you into a cycle of shame. By focusing on improving your work rather than your optics, you're far more likely to achieve better results and a better mindset.

At KeyGlee, our company culture is based on providing growth and support for our employees, but it goes beyond that. We celebrate birthdays, work anniversaries, and new team members who join us (including new additions, like babies). It's not uncommon for some employees to take breaks and walk around our office area. We have First Fridays where we cater food to the office on the first Friday of the month, and sometimes team members will bring in delicious home-baked treats just because.

What gets muddled in the translation of "family culture" is the idea employees are required to hang out with each other—mandating attendance to different company outings, team building, etc. These kinds of mandatory outings and socialization do not make a "family" culture. While we like to think of ourselves as a family, we strive foremost to build a culture of community. As Henry Ford once said, "Coming together is the beginning. Keeping together is progress. Working together is success."

Defining your culture is what pushes you toward long-term success; it's what makes people stay at a company and, if executed poorly, it's what makes employees flee and run for the hills. Community culture is one with a common goal and a purpose. This type of family culture—built on professional respect, collaboration, and community—creates a network that supports the employees and propels the company forward through understanding and celebration. It allows us the space to be human and grow together without judgment.

CORE VALUES

Core values are achievable tenets of culture that you'd like your team to work on consistently. Rather than the technical metrics tied to each position, these operate as metrics that each individual can strive toward. As with culture, core values may not be easily defined in the beginning and will likely evolve as you grow. While you expand your workforce, I'd recommend identifying what qualities you see in your top performers and starting to make those a focus across your entire company.

That said, don't allow these to be vague or cliché values. Even the word "integrity" can have wildly different interpretations to people.

To some, it means never lying; to others, it means sticking to their word; to some, it means not taking that last donut in the break room. Instead, create a term or phrase often used by your team, and craft your own definition so there's no confusion. Get specific and dive into which of your team's qualities are driving the company forward culturally and financially. What about these employees makes them good at their jobs? Don't just look at the surface level, such as how good they are at making money, talking to people, or showing up on time. These are great, but the core goes deeper. An employee who's great at making money might be actually driven toward closing deals or speaking to a certain number of buyers a day, even after their designated work hours. Someone who is good with people might be communicative but also show empathy when speaking to buyers and agents. Your most punctual employee might actually manage their time for projects and other commitments better than anybody else on the team.

Our four core values at KeyGlee are the principles that guide the actions we take in the office and what we carry in our day-to-day lives.

1. **Power Hour**
   - This means having the mindset that you're going to achieve something great today, and you encourage everyone around you to reach those goals. Power Hour is about highlighting the positive things that bring value to your life. We start with our big-picture goals and work backward, designing our lives to achieve them.
   - *Example:* I wake up every day with the belief that I'm going to have a good day and that I'm going to do something great that day. That belief bleeds into my coaching calls with my AstroFlipping community, it bleeds into my filming for *Triple Digit Flip*, and it bleeds into my order at the Starbucks drive-through (tall soy flat white).

2. **#Antlife**
   - Ants refuse to be threatened by the success of others; instead, they work together to achieve their goals because they're stronger together. For us humans, we provide and receive support with the intention to grow and help our

team members grow along with us. We're all just little ants working together to achieve the same goal, so we need to make sure our piece is doing what it should.

- *Example:* I practice #Antlife by not begrudging the success that Josiah or Hunter have brought to KeyGlee, and I certainly don't begrudge the success of any of my competitors; I wish them all the success in the world. The changes we made after trying to scale for the first time laid the foundation of what we used to scale to the business we have today.

3. **Boom, Baby!**
   - This is all about those big wins, whether it's increasing profits or saving the company money. It allows us to grow, set bigger goals, and celebrate when new opportunities are open to us that benefit everyone on the team. The additional financial support allows us to experiment, expand, and explode into our next boom of growth, baby!
   - *Example:* For this, big wins for me are taking the experience I've had and spreading it outward. That growth has opened the doors to incredible opportunities, like being on a variety of podcasts, doing five-hour coaching calls, and attending events across the country.

4. **Cold Showers**
   - Cold showers are about getting out of your comfort zone. A cold shower means pursuing excellence and seeing obstacles as opportunities to overcome. It's seeking out hard work, playing to win, taking responsibility, and not giving up or giving in.
   - *Example:* If I had stayed in my comfort zone after 2008, I would still be drinking and I might have lost my wife; I wouldn't have achieved what I have, and would have lost so much more.

These four core values put into motion across our entire workforce is what has allowed KeyGlee to grow into the nation's largest and fastest-growing wholesale real estate operation. Not only do we look great on paper, but our community, culture, and core values are aligned and practiced daily by our teams across the country. Because of this, we've been awarded a number of accolades, such as winning several placements on *Entrepreneur*'s Franchise 500 List, being invited on various podcasts (including the Motley Fool and BiggerPockets), and getting our own TV show on A&E. We were able to do all of that without having to compromise our ethics because we lived our core values every day and built a strong a company culture.

That carries not only to our more than one hundred franchises, but it's also evident in our sister company, New Reach Education, and in my wholesaling community, AstroFlipping. We built such a strong foundational system that we're able to hand that foundation to other people—like our franchisees—and they're able to scale in the exact same way. Establishing our culture early on enabled us to align our team before we even started to grow.

Step 3: How to Hire the Right People

Your next step is to start hiring people and growing your team. Remember, these are the people who are going to set the foundation for your business because they possess the qualities that you want in future employees.

There are many processes for identifying quality people. Some popular ones are interview questions, personality tests (such as the Big Five traits, which I'll discuss momentarily), and questions geared toward determining if they're a culture fit. Depending on your criteria and the questions you ask, your candidates' responses will give you an idea of where they'll fit into your organization. Be honest. Be curious. Be unafraid to say no.

That said, don't let one or two findings from your hiring process dissuade you from considering someone as a potential employee. For example, just because someone spent an entire Saturday playing a video game or binge-watching Netflix doesn't mean they aren't driven. This is a perfect time to ask more about that weekend—perhaps they were winding down from a stressful week coaching their kid's baseball team or volunteering at a startup. Give your candidates some grace, but don't be afraid to dive deeper.

HIRING'S ROLE IN YOUR BUSINESS TRAJECTORY

One of the largest struggles growing KeyGlee was the hiring process. We were nervous to say no, nervous to say yes, and truthfully, were new to being managers in the first place. It was hard to know why certain hires weren't working out. We weren't sure if it was our leadership style, their skills (or lack thereof), or just the market putting us in a tough spot. Unfortunately, after years of being involved in the company, I've learned it's often (but not always) the person. But that didn't make it easier to let them go once we eliminated all other explanations for their faulty performance. Once we learned how to hire well, ask the right questions, and truly assess if somebody will be a good fit, our growth really started to skyrocket. We were expanding into the Phoenix market and starting to work our way to the top.

After locking in our mission, vision, culture, core values, and improved hiring process for our Phoenix team, we thought we had everything we needed to expand the business into a new location: Las Vegas. We had a small team in Phoenix that was doing great, so we thought we could simply take the success of this team and expand it into a new market. We were wrong.

We made the crucial mistake of trying to do twice as much with the same resources. Our core team was stretched too thin, and while Vegas was struggling to get off the ground, our core operations in Phoenix started to decline as well. Our sales were dropping, our team was burnt out, and the disparate focus was killing us. We ultimately decided to retire our Vegas expansion and refocus on growing in Phoenix. But this "failure" was a blessing in disguise. Refocusing our original operation allowed us to go deeper into the Phoenix market than we even thought possible. We more than doubled our sales—from thirty to over eighty deals in a single month—and made up for the progress we lost in the expansion.

This process isn't uncommon—in fact, this is a commonplace business trajectory. Las Vegas looked like a sensical expansion of our model; after all, if it was working so well in Phoenix, why wouldn't it work in Vegas? But that question was founded on flawed logic. Vegas was a deviation from what made us successful in the first place, and we didn't provide the additional team members, support, and time needed to successfully launch a new branch.

NORMAL BUSINESS TRAJECTORY

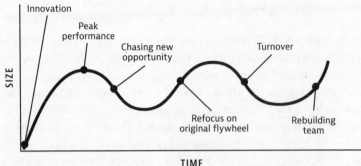

This isn't a new template. In fact, many businesses start this way and continue in this way. It's a business roller coaster, with high peaks and low troughs. In Vegas, we had the same size team as in Phoenix, but they weren't as experienced. To add to that, Vegas is a completely different market than Phoenix, which we didn't appreciate until we tried to expand there. Above all, trying to grow our business in Vegas taught us a few things when it came to hiring the *right* people.

Many new business owners—us included—are nervous to hire. Again, while we had an idea of what our culture and core values would evolve into, we only had a rough blueprint of what our employees would be and what they would need. In Vegas, we needed twice the amount of team members. But a ramp-up in employee numbers raises the question of who will manage them—something we didn't have adequate systems for. We had to build out touchpoints on a quarterly basis and automate processes, but we didn't have an in-house team to do that. We needed managers who could oversee a regular cadence of action item review but who could also coach team members, do performance reviews, and more.

When it comes to expanding a successful business, you can follow the typical trajectory of chasing opportunities and needing to refocus on the basics. But to achieve the trajectory you actually want, you must lock in the innovative gains that come from the foundation of your business.

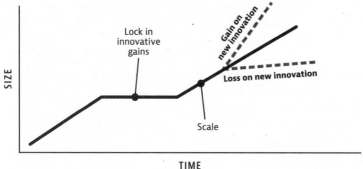

DESIRED BUSINESS TRAJECTORY

Lock in innovative gains

Gain on new innovation

Loss on new innovation

Scale

SIZE

TIME

When we returned to Phoenix (i.e., returned to what was previously working for us), we refocused our efforts on building up our business foundation. This basis carried over to our other locations and our franchises. The people that you hire are the backbone of your business, whether they're working at the forefront or in the background helping the organization thrive. Burning them out on vanity projects, like the Vegas expansion, without the proper resources they needed greatly impacted our success and theirs. However, when we pulled back to Phoenix and rebuilt a more solid foundation, our employees and company thrived more than ever before.

We knew we had a great team, but to really expand, we needed more great people to support that growth. To do this, we started searching for high-potential employees—individuals with an internal drive to succeed who could learn and develop quickly. For us, the key to finding high-potential employees was to hire people for their experience, focusing on those who wanted a career and who wanted to stay at our company because of our approach to innovation and opportunity-spotting. These people were more than employees; they were people who were going to set and build the foundation for our culture. They'd be the example to future employees. This meant that we needed to understand how these employees would grow within the company, such as their potential to be promoted into leadership roles. We also needed to understand what those leadership roles would be and what the path to achieving them looked like.

THE "BIG FIVE" TRAITS

One of the factors we used to determine if these new hires would be a good fit, apart from the actual interview, was an assessment commonly known as the "Big Five." In the 1980s, the scientific community came up with a list of human behaviors that were based on expressions in language and which held some predictive qualities for job performance. Today, people can take the test to determine where they fall on this scale of the main five traits below:

- **O**penness
- **C**onscientiousness
- **E**xtroversion
- **A**greeableness
- **N**euroticism

Openness

This is an obvious one, as it refers to an individual's willingness to be open to new ideas and experiences. In a business environment, this can indicate how open a person is to sharing their own ideas or adopting another's perspective. Within wholesale real estate, some examples would be finding individuals who are open to exploring other markets, testing new marketing approaches, and implementing creative deal structures, all with the goal of finding new solutions to solve a homeowner's pain point profitably.

Conscientiousness

This refers to an individual's ability to be organized, reliable, and responsible. In business, this means being able to manage your time, being detail oriented, and following through on commitments. As a wholesaler, this translates to honest and effective communication with all the stakeholders within a transaction. Sellers, agents, buyers, vendors, and lenders love it when wholesalers perform on their commitments. Conscientiousness also corresponds with someone's proclivity to work hard, which as a wholesaler means working to find leads, speaking to agents, getting deals under contract, and closing those deals.

Extroversion

This usually refers to an individual's ability to be sociable or outgoing. This trait is really based on your specific position. As we talked about in Chapter 7, being an acquisitions or dispositions wholesaler means that you need to speak with buyers, other investors, real estate agents, and vendors repeatedly throughout your day. In contrast, a company's integrator will focus more on systems, technology, and data integration and may go an entire day without having to talk to anyone.

Agreeableness

Agreeableness refers to an individual's tendency to be cooperative, empathetic, and considerate of others. In wholesale, this translates to an individual's capacity to be collaborative. When building out the JV vertical in our business, caring about our partner's profit margins and opportunity costs allows us to make decisions that benefit everyone.

Neuroticism

This trait refers to an individual's level of emotional instability and tendency toward anxiety. For wholesalers, given the high level of stress and delicate situations we deal with on a daily basis, unchecked neuroticism can negatively affect one's decision-making, overall effectiveness, and mental state. Conversely, a healthy level of neuroticism allows you to assess potential future problems, vet opportunities before diving in, and use data to verify your decisions or hesitations rather than gut instinct alone.

These five traits are something that can be used to figure out what type of employee you want to have within your company, but they aren't the be-all and end-all of what you should look for as you hire.

When we refocused on building up the Phoenix office, we first looked for somebody with a high level of conscientiousness (meaning they're driven to achieve their goals), closely followed by agreeableness and openness. But keep in mind that while someone might match all of the traits you're looking for, that may not correlate to them being a cultural fit. There are a number of other factors that come into play once they actually are hired that might impact their effectiveness and fit at your company.

For example, employees who don't feel appreciated will be less inclined to do the work that is required of them, and they'll be less inclined to do that work with you. In 2022, a report from Gallup[5] showed that only 32 percent of employees were actively engaged in their jobs. That equates to 68 percent of employees who are disengaged at work, which can cost a company $3,400 for every $10,000 they make. And this isn't a new problem—2022 isn't the first year that employees have reported their dissatisfaction with their employers or work environment.

We wanted to avoid that by making sure that everyone we extended an offer to had all of the elements they need to succeed, whether that's culture fit, personality, or skills. We made sure to have a fully functional human resources (HR) department that would provide any help or guidance to our employees. We have weekly check-ins with team members to understand what their goals are (both in and out of the workplace) or to address any challenges or roadblocks they might be having. And we provide benefits to ensure our employees and their families are healthy and stay healthy.

The reason we do this is that these fulfilled, engaged employees are the ones who stay with the company and grow to be leaders within the company.

WHOM TO HIRE: QUALITIES OF AN ENTREPRENEUR

At the risk of sounding repetitive, the people you hire can, in many cases, make or break your business. Hiring the wrong people means the work you need done isn't getting done, your entire team's dynamic can be thrown off track, and it can even cost you and your company thousands of dollars due to turnover, ineffectiveness, or even theft. When it comes to determining if you've found the right person or not, there are a few ways to identify this. As I mentioned, KeyGlee often uses the Big Five traits to get an initial idea of where they may align with our culture and values. There are several other ways you

---

5   https://www.zippia.com/advice/employee-engagement-statistics/

can continue to learn more about a prospective employee, including the kind of questions you ask in the interview. Here are some of my favorite questions to ask:

- What do you do on Saturdays/did you do last Saturday?
- Where do you get your moral code or compass from?
- Who is your favorite person you have ever worked with or for, and why?
- Who is your least favorite person you have ever worked with, and why?
- When was the last text message you got that you didn't respond to?
- What is something interesting you learned recently about the industry?

For example, asking a potential team member what they do on a Saturday can give you an idea of high consciousness. If they say something along the lines of taking classes or spending time with family, that could be a signal of someone who is driven toward their own goals of success and who has strong core values. Someone who just plays video games all day isn't necessarily "not driven enough to hire," but they may not have the same passionate, go-getter attitude as the first candidate. Don't get me wrong, video games and relaxation aren't an immediate red flag—we all need that. And one answer to a question like this shouldn't necessarily make or break a potential hire; rather, it should work in combination as part of a larger picture of the life they live and who they are inside and outside of work. If they align with your culture, great! If not, then keep looking.

Keep in mind that you ultimately want to hire people for experience and the value they can add to your company long term. It's also helpful to look for people seeking a career, not just their next job. Some people might think a job *is* a career, but it's not. I'm going to totally sound like a parent right now, but a job is something you have to fulfill a specific purpose. For most of us, a job is the work obligation we have in exchange for spending money for food, entertainment, boyfriends/girlfriends, a car, whatever; it's the thing we do because we have to. Having a career, however, is usually a long-term commitment. It's a professional journey that gives you growth in a particular industry or field.

When I started working at a media company in 2002, I didn't think that would be a career. It was the paycheck I needed to keep a roof over my head and put food in my stomach. It was a means to an end. Of course, at the time, I had no idea that being at that company would lead me to the career I'm in now—that can happen! There are many people who started with a job and then found themselves on another path that led them to their professional career now.

When we looked at the people we wanted in our company, we wanted people who had all the *elements* to be a successful entrepreneur, but instead of running their own company, they wanted to grow within ours. We did this because entrepreneurs want to take control of their own businesses. That's great; that's why you're reading this book! However, in a business setting, you want employees who aren't gunning to replace the CEO or become your next biggest competition. The candidates you're looking for will feel fulfilled strengthening their team and company's foundation and providing the personal perspective and skills to move your company forward.

Step 4: Establish an Organizational Structure

When people think of structure within an organization, they often think it means creating a bureaucracy, layers of "red tape," and corporate politics. The problem with this thinking is that leaders can be so fearful of creating a bureaucracy that they lose the ability to manage all the communication pathways between employees and, eventually, departments. So what, exactly, is the difference between the bureaucracy and structure?

STRUCTURE VERSUS BUREAUCRACY

Structure refers to the way a company arranges its departments, teams, roles, and responsibilities to determine how the flow of information, resources, and authority gets to those who need it. Bureaucracy refers to a specific type of organizational structure that incorporates a clear division of labor and is usually characterized by having a hierarchy, rigid rules, and centralized control. Think of structure as the broad concept of how a company organizes its various components to achieve its business goals. While bureaucracy is a specific type of organizational structure, it often leads to inefficiencies and reduced flexibility. Many large corporations might run their organizations as a bureaucracy; however, we certainly don't at KeyGlee, and I don't recommend you do either.

The key to building a structure without instituting a bureaucracy is the foundation you put in place for what you want your business to do and how you'll achieve those goals. For us, the foundation focused on three key elements:

- People
- Strategy
- Operations

These things will look different if you're running a one-person business, and that's okay. Many business owners start out as the head and employee of every department. But at some point, as your business begins to grow, the business will need more people. A general rule of thumb is to ensure that you have managerial positions once you have more than four employees, but you assign no more than eight employees to one manager. Different departments will have different requirements, depending on what their needs are. For example, a sales department may have twelve people to one manager.

When it comes to managing, keep the delegation rule top of mind. If an employee or team member can do the task 70 percent as well as you could, then as a manager, you should delegate that responsibility to that employee. This means assigning specific tasks to your team that you, as a manager, shouldn't be doing and will otherwise eat into time that could be spent on more important projects. For example, if you are the manager of a sales department, you should be delegating the task of calling clients or customers to other members in your department, while you analyze reports, review data, or craft strategy. In order to delegate tasks, you need to have a team that is qualified in those positions. This is where finding and keeping talent comes in.

When we switched our focus from the Phoenix market to Las Vegas, we discovered that the latter market was a distraction. This doesn't mean that we abandoned our efforts in Vegas or we never returned—we eventually did—it just means that starting a new business location distracted us from what was working in the first business location. As I mentioned earlier, we decided to put our efforts in Vegas on hold and refocused on Phoenix, going much deeper into setting up our business structure in a more streamlined way. This resulted in us being able to double our deal flow within the business. Once we understood the model we have now, we began to focus more on our company structure and how to organize our people in that structure. That meant putting standard operating procedures (SOPs) in place for our management and leadership teams, and knowing what daily numbers and metrics we wanted to hit. In the beginning, we were unsure of how many calls we needed our acquisitions and dispositions team members to make on a daily basis, but once we learned which metrics made sense for us and would help us achieve the goals and targets we had set, *then* we could start looking at other markets. The model we finally put in place, understood, and executed is what led us to branch out into the markets of Orlando, Tampa, Atlanta, Boise, Tucson, Dallas, Austin, Houston, Jacksonville, and yes, Las Vegas.

HOW TO ORGANIZE YOUR PEOPLE

There are two different types of structure: functional structure and mission-based structure. Most small to medium-sized businesses start out using a functional structure. Functional structure is divided into specialized groups with specific roles and duties. This might be Finance, HR, or a Sales team. The function is in their names. In mission-based structures, their objectives are focused on value multipliers and are usually reserved for need-based, critical, or urgent issues or opportunities. Any type of environmental business might have a mission-based structure because they often work toward human health, air, land, and water issues.

KeyGlee uses a combination of both functional and mission-based structure. Our company is set up with separate departments for acquisitions, dispositions, title and escrow, finance, and HR and talent acquisitions, with a focus on the disciplines of the people in that department (functional) and a focus for our franchisees in particular markets (mission-based). Below is an example of a generic, functional structure of a bookkeeping organization:

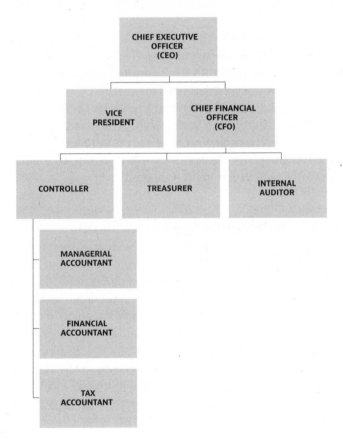

Mission-based structure, on the other hand, would involve having a focus on a particular community goal or outcome across departments. At KeyGlee, our mission-based structure is focused on the particular market that we're located in, such as Phoenix or Las Vegas.

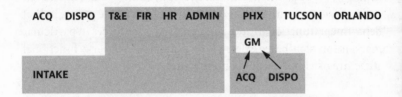

We've combined both functional and mission-based structures to ensure that all of our departments and locations are aligned across the entire business. Again, it's about putting people in positions that match the skills you need. Just like I'm not the CEO of KeyGlee due to Josiah (and then later Hunter) having skills that I lacked, the ability to build a team that reflects your mission, vision, culture, and core values starts with having great people to create that team. But how do you recognize that talent? How do you measure performance so you have the right people in the right positions?

Step 5: Determine How to Measure Success

Now that you have a unified team and a structure for their reporting, you need to determine if they're generating the results your company needs. Your first question might be "How do I measure the success of my team?" You might think this is the most important question and the one you should spend the most time on. But it's not. In fact, the question you should ask is "Why should I measure the success of my team at all?"

For the most part, the purpose of measuring the success of your team is to identify areas of improvement; ultimately, you'll want to use these to create achievable targets, goals, and metrics. Let me explain what each of these are and what they're for.

- **Targets.** Targets are set by the business and are based on what a particular role needs and what needs to be delivered in order to achieve that target. A target for a general manager, for example, can be something like "Achieve $50,000 in profit over two years." Targets should be based on a historic model and should be achievable.

- **Goals.** Goals can be whatever you want the business or your team members to accomplish. Again, these need to be achievable, but it doesn't mean they can't be lofty. Business-wise, a goal might be expanding your business to another city or state, but you can also have personal goals, like wanting to visit another country or saving a certain amount of money for retirement.
- **Metrics.** Metrics, sometimes known as key performance indicators (KPIs), track how effectively a team member, team, or company is achieving a particular business objective. These KPIs can should be measurable, such as profit margin growth, cash flow, or organic traffic.

These measurements can vary from business to business, but they are an important aspect that you should incorporate in yours. With the correct measurements, you can see the growth trajectory of your business and individual teams.

Another way to measure success is by having meetings to align on projects and remove any roadblocks preventing that progress. I know, I know—meetings can sometimes feel like the biggest waste of time. But an effective, efficient meeting can be incredibly beneficial. Here's how KeyGlee sets up our meetings:

TYPES OF MEETINGS

Type	Purpose	Group Size	Duration	Style	Interactions
Stand-up	Pass information	Small	Short time	Quick update	Transmit
Status update	Single focus/ update	Small-mid	Cap at an hour	Agenda based	Updates
Staff meeting	Multi dept. updates Disseminate updates	Small-mid	Cap at an hour	Project/ dept. updates Agenda based	Some Each person has an update
Touch base	Interactive update Personal or professional	Small	15-60 min	Agenda	High

Impromptu	Decision or discussion	Small	Short	No agenda	Moderate-high
Brainstorming	Solicit ideas	Small	Managed time	Facilitated	High participation, less debate
Discussion	Drive alignment/ explore Some updates	Small-mid	Open	Facilitated	High
Decision meeting	Leave meeting with decision	Mid	Open	Facilitated	High debate
Info sharing	Broadly disseminate idea/ decision	Small-large	Cap at an hour	Single speaker	Transmit

These meetings are intended to be productive and to pass along information or updates within the company. The best way to do this is to keep them short and focused, and to provide clear outlines as to what you want to achieve in each meeting.

As you're starting out, you may only have a small team, so your "stand-up" might be incorporated into your staff meetings. As you can see, the only large meetings are for info-sharing and decision-making. Once you've grown to have between eight and ten people on staff, your meeting types should change. At KeyGlee, we have weekly 1:1s between team members and their team leader or manager; this is where they discuss different performance metrics, what management needs from their team members, what the employee needs from their manager/leader, and any additional coaching or training to achieve their goals. We also have weekly meetings for our department heads so we can review each department's performance. This helps us see where each department is and where they might need help.

Meetings *can* be boring if there's no reasoning behind why they're being held or if there's no benefit to those involved in them. This is why having organizational structure is so crucial. With a strong structure, you can easily identify key players at each level, prioritize who should attend which meetings, and ensure they're all aligned in their shared goals and vision. Meetings don't have to be the enemy or unnecessary; they can be used to relay important information about a team member's goals—whether professional or personal—review what each department is doing and why, and regularly measure progress.

Step 6: Scale Your Business

This chapter has looked at how KeyGlee was able to scale according to the path we set. One of the most important things we learned on this journey was to never fully abandon what brought us success in the first place. Our Phoenix office, the first one in the KeyGlee chain, had a phenomenal amount of success, to the point where we immediately thought we should expand to other markets. That turned out to be a misstep for us because we didn't have a structure in place yet to successfully repeat that success in other locations. Once we reflected on our mistakes and grew our workforce and structure in Phoenix—along with our mission, vision, core values, and culture—we were able to recreate that original success several times over. We expanded into Orlando, Tampa, Atlanta, Boise, Dallas, Austin, and eventually back into Vegas. KeyGlee and our franchises now operate in over one hundred markets nationwide.

There's the old adage of "If it ain't broke, don't fix it." In some cases, this saying is justified; we have a system now that only grows stronger each day, with each new team member and each new location. That doesn't mean you can't—or shouldn't—tweak things as you grow, especially if those tweaks will further your business's success without compromising ethics, honesty, or values.

Another key component when it comes to scaling is staying plugged into the industry. It's important to understand what's happening in your market, who your competitors are, what they're doing in the space, and what emerging markets are ideal for expansion. Having this information means you're better equipped to know what's happening not just in your own backyard, but all around you. And remember, as you collect more information and experience, make sure you're sharing it! It truly is not going to hurt you to share your wealth of knowledge and provide value to others—whether it's posting on Facebook, talking on the phone with a friend, or writing a whole book. We've all started at the bottom at one point, so be sure to share your journey with others along with any tips and tricks you've learned along the way. If you do this consistently enough, especially on social media, you may even grow a following and expand your reach! Don't be afraid to share every form of success—whether you're featured in an article, do an interview or podcast, or get a spotlight in your local paper. This type of PR boosts your and your company's exposure, so use it. Just remember to always strive to add value.

The last thing I want to leave you with in this chapter are other resources where you can get great business advice. As the host of a few podcasts, I can absolutely say these are fantastic and free ways to get business advice and ideas on how to build and scale your business. Podcasts are probably the quickest and easiest way to learn—you can listen in the car, while mowing the lawn, working out, and so on. The BiggerPockets *On the Market* podcast is a great resource on current trends in the real estate landscape. BiggerPockets also has several other amazing podcasts, such as their *Real Estate* podcast, *Money* podcast, *Rookie* podcast, and the *InvestHER* podcast. Other great podcasts are *Wholesaling Inc.* and *Real Estate Rockstars*.

Above all else, however, remember that growing your business is a journey, and there are many different ways you can shape that path. Several decades ago, I stumbled into real estate investing, and even with economic crashes, downward spirals, and failed expansions, it's been one of the most fulfilling adventures I've ever had that I never even knew I wanted.

Conclusion

In this book, we have explored the world of wholesaling through my twenty-plus years of experience within the real estate industry. You've learned the fundamentals of wholesaling, the key principles that underpin it, and the best practices that successful wholesalers follow. Additionally, I've shared with you the challenges that I've faced, along with the proper approaches that allow you to find "once in a lifetime" opportunities weekly. We have learned that wholesaling is not just about buying and selling real estate at a profit. It is about building relationships, understanding client needs, and delivering value through efficient and effective action plans and property assessment. We have also learned that success in wholesaling requires a strong work ethic, a passion for the business, and a willingness to take calculated risks. My persistence, discipline, and attention to detail helped me overcome the 2008 crisis and eventually develop the amazing team at KeyGlee. Thank goodness everything worked out after 2008. I was tired of bombing onstage at Los Angeles comedy clubs!

Wholesaling is a complex and multifaceted field that requires a diverse range of skills and knowledge. It is not something that can be mastered overnight; rather, it's a multi-year journey that requires ongoing learning, adaptation, and growth. That said, even if you're brand-new to real estate or you're an agent aspiring to be a wholesaler, the insights and strategies shared in this book will help you navigate the ever-changing landscape of the wholesale industry and succeed in your business endeavors.

As I've said repeatedly, adopting a powerful mindset will change your life. You have a connection with every human being in this world in some form or capacity. Change the way you think, feel, and act according to the person you *want* to become. Inevitably, the right people will be drawn to your life. One of the most incredible phenomena I've experienced is how people and opportunities naturally arrange themselves around those with pure intentions to produce the highest and best benefit for all. In other words, good things happen to good people, and good people attract *other* good people. I'm so grateful to have played a role in the evolution of wholesaling into an ethical and accessible real estate investing strategy. A decade ago, wholesalers hid in the shadows, ashamed of being the "lowly" starting point of an investor's journey. Today, we're having television shows made about us.

To say the rise in popularity has been meteoric is an understatement. Along with this attention and interest comes an incredible opportunity to redefine the value that wholesaling has to communities, businesses, and struggling individuals looking for a way into an industry that has created so many millionaires. I remember exactly how it felt in the beginning, when it seemed as though I had no way in. While I didn't invent wholesaling, I can proudly say I am part of the movement that's kicked the f**ing door down for everyone. So there you have it—the door's open, and the steps to success are in your hands. This business will never be done alone.

In case you're wondering where to find me, I can be found on Instagram as @jdamji. I read all comments, so please feel free to shout out that you bought this book along with what you learned from it. I'm also on BiggerPockets via YouTube and would love to engage with you there on everything wholesaling.

Until next time, keep reaching your maximum potential, and align your thoughts and actions toward the person you will become. Treat people with integrity and respect—the universe will serve you the same way. I'll see you around, and let's make some life-changing deals happen.

Acknowledgments

I must acknowledge my incredible team who always, always show up for me! Bobby Kanode, Emily Voght, and Yvette Mackenzie—you guys are world class. I'm sorry I stress you all out. Thanks for keeping up with my craziness and helping me grow this movement.

To all the staff at KeyGlee and New Reach Education—we built the greatest wholesale company in the world and then shared our knowledge with everyone we could. I'm so grateful you all wake up every day with love in your heart and serve people as tirelessly as you do.

To the incredible folks at A&E Networks—thanks for putting our work into the world! We are inspiring millions.

To the wonderful editing and publishing staff at BiggerPockets—thanks for taking a chance on me and this book. I hope we sell a bunch of copies. I love you!

To my *On the Market* crew—I enjoy every minute we have together (and that James Dainard always pays the bill).

Lastly, to my writing team—Jacob Rothenberg, Elliot Charland, and Regina R Woodard—we all worked so hard together for so many hours. This accomplishment is as much yours as it is mine. Thanks, and I love you all.

Glossary of Terms

A-B contract
An A-B contract is between the buyer and seller that opens the first escrow on a property. There are three different purposes for an A-B contract: putting the property under contract to purchase, putting it under contract to wholesale, and protecting the side of the buyer.

Acquisition wholesaling
The process of gaining ownership or control of real property. Also called wholesale acquisitions.

After repair value (ARV)
The estimate of potential value of a property after all repairs or renovations have been made.

Appraisal rules
The comparison of a subject property to three to six similar neighborhood homes. Dollar adjustments are made for physical or amenity differences.

Appraiser
An individual who estimates the value of land or buildings, usually before they are sold, purchased, mortgaged, taxed, insured, or

developed. Appraisers will routinely conduct a thorough inspection of a property to assess its true worth.

Also see **Inspection period** *and* **Appraisal rules.**

Appreciation
The increase of value for a house or investment property that happens over a period of time. Raised values can lead to profits for the home-owner or seller upon selling the home or property. Appreciation also increases the home's equity.

Also see **Equity.**

Assignment contract
An assignment contract is the transfer of position of one party in a contract to another party. Prevalent in real estate investing when it comes to contracting a property for wholesaling and fix-and-flip deals.

B-C contract
A B-C contract is written to protect the seller (Person B in an A-B contract) during the process of a property sale; frequently used when selling a wholesale property to another investor or buyer (Person C) to create a new escrow.

Cash buyer
An individual who uses their own funds to cover the full purchase price of a home or property. These funds do not come from a loan, but instead come from savings, investments, or the sale of another property or home. Also known just as a buyer.

Comping
From the term "comparable," comping is the act of comparing prop-erties or homes within a selected area against another property, usu-ally during the process of buying or selling a property.

Consumer protection agencies

Consumer protection agencies are governmental authorities that regulate, administer, or enforce consumer protection laws. This includes stopping the unfair, deceptive, and fraudulent business practices by collecting reports from consumers and conducting investigations on reported businesses and companies.

Also see the **Federal Communications Commission** *and* **TCPA**.

Contract clause

A provision or condition that specifies rights, duties, or obligations of all parties involved in the signing of a contract.

Creative financing

Uncommon or unique ways for an individual to purchase land or properties for sale. The goal is generally to purchase or finance a property using little or no money from the buyer or investor.

Also see **Subject-to** *and* **Seller finance**.

Deal

In wholesale real estate, a deal is a short-term investment strategy used by investors to realize fast profits in a short amount of time. A deal can come from a variety of sources, typically through a seller, a buyer, or a combination of both.

Deed of trust

An agreement between a home buyer and a lender at the closing of a property and held by a third party—usually a bank, title company, or escrow company—and used as collateral for the promissory note. Deeds of trust are sometimes used in place of a mortgage.

Disposition wholesaling

The process of selling the equitable interest in a property that has been put under contract. Also called wholesale dispositions.

Distressed property
A property or home that is on the brink of foreclosure or has already been bought back by the bank. In many cases, the sellers of these properties are unable to provide the financial resources required to invest in repairs.

Distressed seller/Distressed situation
An individual or individuals who need to sell an asset urgently. In many cases, the seller needs to pay off debts, medical expenses, or other unforeseen emergencies that require them to sell an asset, usually property, in a faster manner than traditional real estate sales.

Also see **Distressed property**.

Double escrow
A set of real estate transactions involving two contracts of sale for the same property, two different back-to-back buyers, at the same or two different prices, arranged to close on the same date.

Down market
In real estate terminology, a down market is when the inventory for housing is low and pricing begins to drop.

Earnest money deposit (EMD)
The sum of money that a buyer puts down to demonstrate their seriousness about buying a property or home.

Equity
The value of financial interest in a home. Homeowner equity is usually the share of the home that is owned by the homeowner; that is, the value of the home rather than what is owed on the mortgage.

Federal Communications Commission
The U.S. government agency that regulates interstate and international communications through cable, radio, television, satellite, and wire.

Foreclosure
The process by which a lender repossesses a house or property as security or collateral for a loan; that is, the lender obtains ownership of the home or property.

Hard money lender (HML)
A type of secured loan that is used to buy hard assets, usually real estate. Lenders are typically either a company or an individual who weighs the merit of a property investment and uses that as collateral.

Homeowner association (HOA) lien
A homeowner association lien is a legal claim or hold on a piece of property within an associated neighborhood. It is the association's legal claim to an owner's property.

Inspection period
The time period for an inspection or review of a property or home by an inspector. The inspection period ranges from one to thirty calendar days. The buyer pays for the inspection.

Joint venture (JV)
A business arrangement or partnership in which two or more parties agree to work together on a specific project or business venture. Parties involved typically contribute resources, such as money, equipment, or property, and they share in both profits and losses of the venture.

Judgment
A judgment or judgment lien gives a creditor the right to be paid a certain amount of money from proceeds from the sale of a debtor's property.

Lead
A prospective motivated seller.

Maximum allowable offer (MAO)
The highest purchase amount an investor can offer on a house while still making their desired profit.

Mechanic lien
A legal tool that provides an unpaid party with a security interest in the property. Contractors and suppliers mostly use these.

Multiple listing service (MLS)
A resource tool to help listing agents and brokers find other cooperative agents and brokers who are working with buyers to sell their clients' properties or homes. Created by the National Association of Realtors® to help level the playing field for Realtors.

National Association of Realtors (NAR)®
Founded in 1908 as the National Association of Real Estate Exchanges, the NAR is one of the largest trade associations in the United States. The NAR has over 1.5 million members, 54 state associations, and more than 1,000 local associations. Members include residential and commercial brokers, salespeople, property managers, appraisers, counselors, and others within the real estate industry.

Option contract
An agreement that allows the buyer to purchase a property from a seller within a specific timeframe and at a specific price.

Private money lender (PML)
Private individuals or companies that lend money to investors. In many cases, a private money lender is someone who is close to the investor or buyer, such as a family member or friend. However, there are also PMLs who lend money without previous affiliation with the investor.

Real estate agent
A licensed professional who represents buyers or sellers in real estate transactions.

Real estate investor
An individual who invests capital in real estate property by buying and selling properties.

Realtor
A licensed professional who acts as an agent for the sale and purchase of buildings and land. They are generally members of the National Association of Realtors®. It is always spelled with a capital R.

Also see **National Association of Realtors®**.

Rehab
A real estate rehab is when investors purchase a property, complete renovations, and then sell the property for a profit.

Rehabber
A person who conducts a rehab on a property.

Relocation
The process of leaving one place for another. Usually used when describing a move of a considerable distance.

Seller
An individual who sells a property or home.

Seller finance
A situation in which a seller agrees to take a set payment on a regular basis from a buyer on a property. The buyer purchases the property and pays the seller their requested sell price, usually on a payment schedule, such as monthly or biweekly.

Also see **Creative financing** *and* **Subject-to**.

Skip trace/Skip tracing
The process of looking for property owners, prospects, or property leads by using their known address.

Square footage
The measurement of living space of a property in square feet.

Subdivision
In terms of real estate, it is a smaller area within a neighborhood.

Subject-to
A situation in which a buyer agrees to take over the existing mortgage on a property without transferring that mortgage into their name. The buyer instead makes payments to the lender as agreed, but the seller continues to be the legal responsible party of that property.

Also see **Creative financing** *and* **Seller finance**.

Tax record
Any documentation relating to any tax claims that support income, expenses, and credits reported.

Telephone Consumer Protection Act (TCPA)
The TCPA was enacted in 1991 to control telemarketing calls, automatic telephone dialing systems, and artificial or prerecorded voice messages.

Also see **Federal Communications Commission**.

Transactional funding
A type of real estate loan that allows you to buy and sell real estate using the same funding source

Wholesale real estate
Wholesale real estate is a form of real estate investing where we're acting as a principal in a transaction.

Also see **Wholesaler**.

Wholesaler

An individual who invests in real estate by wholesaling.

Also see **Wholesale real estate**.

Works Cited

Adelman, J. (2020, November 19). *New city law aims to crack down on real estate 'wholesalers', seen as exploiting underinformed property owners.* Retrieved from The Philadelphia Inquirer: https://www.inquirer.com/news/real-estate-wholesalers-flippers-regulation-realtors-philadelphia-law-20201119.html

Altmann, D. M., and R. J. Boyton. (2022, March 10). *COVID-19 vaccination: The road ahead.* Retrieved from Science.org: https://www.science.org/doi/10.1126/science.abn1755

Appraiser Career Center. "Knowledge Base." http://www.appraiser-career.com/knowledgebase/

Beech, I. (2023, March 1). *9 famous joint venture examples.* Retrieved from Breezy: https://breezy.io/blog/joint-venture-examples

BiggerPockets. "Advanced Rehab Cost Estimator." http://biggerpockets.com/rehab-estimator.

Bunting, L. (2022, March 17). *Equitable interest important factor | Real Estate Report.* Retrieved from OC Today, https://www.oceancitytoday.com/business/real_estate_report/equitable-interest-important-factor/article_8048b9c4-a624-11ec-b7fe-e3f1c95c4247.html

Contact Center Compliance. (n.d.). *What is the TCPA?* Retrieved from Contact Center Compliance: https://www.dnc.com/what-is-tcpa

Cox, J. (2022, June 15). *Fed hikes its benchmark interest rate by 0.75 percentage point, the biggest increase since 1994.* Retrieved from CNBC: https://www.cnbc.com/2022/06/15/fed-hikes-its-benchmark-interest-rate-by-three-quarters-of-a-point-the-biggest-increase-since-1994.html

Damji, J. "AstroFlipping." AstroFlipping: Real Estate Education, New Reach Education, https://www.astroflipping.com/

Facebook. "AstroFlipping Public Group." https://www.facebook.com/groups/astroflippingpublic

Federal Trade Commission. (2009, September). *CAN-SPAM Act: A Compliance Guide for Business.* Retrieved from Federal Trade Commission: https://www.ftc.gov/business-guidance/resources/can-spam-act-compliance-guide-business

Ferry, M. (2018). *Quiet Mind Epic Life: Escape the Status Quo & Experience Enlightened Prosperity Now.* Independently published.

Flipping Mastery TV. (2022, January 7). *Real Estate Wholesaling Regulations in 2022.* Retrieved from YouTube.com: https://www.youtube.com/watch?v=9KgwoYlh2CA

Frankel, L. (2022, August 1). *Rising Interest Rates Challenge Investors —Here's What Expert Lenders Suggest You Do.* Retrieved from BiggerPockets: https://www.biggerpockets.com/blog/rising-interest-rates-challenge-investors

Gong, Z. et al. (2022, July 7). *The Relationship Between Academic Encouragement and Academic Self-Efficacy: A Moderated Mediation Model.* Retrieved from Frontiers in Psychology: https://www.frontiersin.org/articles/10.3389/fpsyg.2022.644243/full

Hargreaves, L. (2020, January 20). *California Now Requires Reporting of All Real Estate Sales.* Retrieved from Worldwide ERC: https://www.worldwideerc.org/news/public-policy/california-now-requires-reporting-of-all-real-estate-sales

Hopkins, D. *Bullseye Branding Bullseye Branding: Home - Video,* http://bullseyebranding.com.

KPMG. (2022, March). *Six key trends impacting global supply chains in 2022.* Retrieved from KPMG: https://home.kpmg/sg/en/home/insights/2022/03/six-key-trends-impacting-global-supply-chains-in-2022.html

Lovelace, B. (2022, September 16). *1 in 5 households has medical debt. That includes people with private insurance.* Retrieved from NBC News: https://www.nbcnews.com/health/health-news/1-5-households-medical-debt-includes-people-private-insurance-rcna48076

Mannheimer, S. (2022, December 11). *SMS Marketing Statistics 2022 for USA Businesses.* Retrieved from SMS comparison: https://www.smscomparison.com/mass-text-messaging/2022-statistics/

National Real Estate Wholesalers Association. (n.d.). Retrieved from National Real Estate Wholesalers Assocation: https://nrewa.org/

New York State Department of State. (2021, March). *Real Estate Broker Overview.* Retrieved from New York State Department of State: https://dos.ny.gov/real-estate-broker

Perlman, E. (2022, May 2). *How the Russia-Ukraine War Can Impact the U.S. Housing Market.* Retrieved from LinkedIn: https://www.linkedin.com/pulse/how-russia-ukraine-war-can-impact-us-housing-market-ellie-perlman?trk=pulse-article

Petronella, L. *Cost of Becoming an Arizona Real Estate Salesperson.* *AceableAgent,* https://www.aceableagent.com/blog/cost-becoming-arizona-real-estate-salesperson/

Sackrin & Tolchinsky, P.A., Attorneys at Law. (2016, June 28). *Can a Buyer Assign or Transfer Rights in Florida Real Property to Third Person Before Closing?* Retrieved from About Florida Law: https://aboutfloridalaw.com/2016/06/28/can-a-buyer-assign-or-transfer-rights-in-florida-real-property-to-third-person-before-closing/

Syrios, A. (2022, December 15). *The "Sellers Strike" Has Begun— Why the Housing Market Is Going Dark.* Retrieved from BiggerPockets: https://www.biggerpockets.com/blog/the-sellers-strike-has-begun-why-the-housing-market-is-going-dark

Thorsby, D. (2022, November 10). *What Is a Housing Market Price Correction?* Retrieved from U.S. News - Real Estate: https://realestate.usnews.com/real-estate/articles/what-is-a-housing-market-price-correction

Webber, M. R. (2022, August 31). *Deed of Trust: Meaning, How it Works, Benefits.* Retrieved from Investopedia: https://www.investopedia.com/deed-of-trust-definition-5221503

Wholesale Hotline. (n.d.). Retrieved from YouTube: https://www.youtube.com/@wholesalehotline9431/streams

Workable. (2023, March 2) *Real Estate Broker job description.* Workable resources, https://resources.workable.com/real-estate-broker-job-description

More from
BiggerPockets Publishing

Wealth without Cash: Supercharge Your Real Estate Investing with Subject-to, Seller Financing, and Other Creative Deals

Creative deals are the fastest and cheapest way to supercharge your real estate investment portfolio, and Pace Morby—TV host of A&E's *Triple Digit Flip* and a real estate investing influencer with more than a million followers—will guide you through these innovative strategies. From seller finance and subject-to, creative finance helped him acquire more than 1,000 properties and $150 million in assets without using his own cash. Whether you're just getting started as an investor or already have a real estate business, this book will fully prepare you to find off-market leads, uncover sellers' motivations, negotiate with confidence, close more deals, build a team, and much more.

The Book on Estimating Rehab Costs

Learn detailed tips, tricks, and tactics to accurately budget nearly any house flipping project from expert fix-and-flipper J Scott. Whether you are preparing to walk through your very first rehab project or you're an experienced home flipper, this handbook will be your guide to identifying renovation projects, creating a scope of work, and staying on budget to ensure a timely profit!

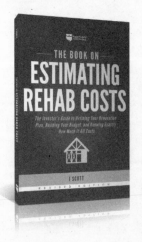

If you enjoyed this book, we hope you'll take a moment to check out some of the other great material BiggerPockets offers. Whether you crave freedom or stability, a backup plan, or passive income, BiggerPockets empowers you to live life on your own terms through real estate investing. Find the information, inspiration, and tools you need to dive right into the world of real estate investing with confidence.

Sign up today—it's free! Visit www.BiggerPockets.com
Find our books at www.BiggerPockets.com/store

The Book on Tax Strategies for the Savvy Real Estate Investor

Taxes! Boring and irritating, right? Perhaps. But if you want to succeed in real estate, your tax strategy will play a huge role in how fast you grow. A great tax strategy can save you thousands of dollars a year. A bad strategy could land you in legal trouble. With *The Book on Tax Strategies for the Savvy Real Estate Investor*, you'll find ways to deduct more, invest smarter, and pay far less to the IRS!

The Intention Journal

Some people can achieve great wealth, rock-solid relationships, age-defying health, and remarkable happiness—and so many others struggle, fail, and give up on their dreams, goals, and ambitions. Could it simply be that those who find success are more intentional about it? Once you build intentionality into your daily routine, you can achieve the incredible success that sometimes seems out of reach. Backed by the latest research in psychology, this daily planner offers an effective framework to set, review, and accomplish your goals.

Looking for more?
Join the BiggerPockets Community

BiggerPockets brings together education, tools, and a community of more than 2+ million like-minded members— all in one place. Learn about investment strategies, analyze properties, connect with investor-friendly agents, and more.

Go to **biggerpockets.com** to learn more!

 Listen to a **BiggerPockets Podcast**

 Watch **BiggerPockets on YouTube**

 Join the **Community Forum**

 Learn more on **the Blog**

 Read more **BiggerPockets Books**

 Learn about our **Real Estate Investing Bootcamps**

 Connect with an **Investor-Friendly Real Estate Agent**

 Go Pro! Start, scale, and manage your portfolio with your **Pro Membership**

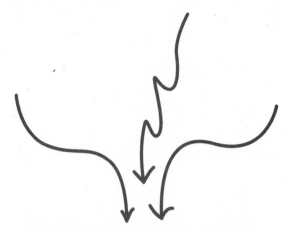

Follow us on social media!

Sign up for a Pro account
and take **20 PERCENT OFF**
with code **BOOKS20**.